**OLD MOORE'S**

# Horoscope and Astral Diary

## VIRGO

**OLD MOORE'S**

# HOROSCOPE AND ASTRAL DIARY

# VIRGO

foulsham
LONDON • NEW YORK • TORONTO • SYDNEY

foulsham
The Old Barrel Store, Drayman's Lane, Marlow, Bucks SL7 2FF

Foulsham books can be found in all good bookshops and direct from www.foulsham.com

ISBN: 978-0-572-04501-2



A CIP record for this book is available from the British Library



Typeset in Great Britain by Chris Brewer Origination, Christchurch
Printed in Great Britain by Martins The Printers, Berwick-upon-Tweed

# CONTENTS

# INTRODUCTION

Astrology has been a part of life for centuries now, and no matter how technological our lives become, it seems that it never diminishes in popularity. For thousands of years people have been gazing up at the star-clad heavens and seeing their own activities and proclivities reflected in the movement of those little points of light. Across centuries countless hours have been spent studying the way our natures, activities and decisions seem to be paralleled by their predictable movements. Old Moore, a time-served veteran in astrological research, continues to monitor the zodiac and has produced the Astral Diary for 2015, tailor-made to your own astrological makeup.

*Old Moore's Astral Diary* is unique in its ability to get the heart of your nature and to offer you the sort of advice that might come from a trusted friend. It enables you to see in a day-by-day sense exactly how the planets are working for you. The diary section advises how you can get the best from upcoming situations and allows you to plan ahead successfully. There's also room on each daily entry to record your own observations or appointments.

While other popular astrology books merely deal with your astrological 'Sun sign', the Astral Diaries go much further. Every person on the planet is unique and Old Moore allows you to access your individuality in a number of ways. The front section gives you the chance to work out the placement of the Moon at the time of your birth and to see how its position has set an important seal on your overall nature. Perhaps most important of all, you can use the Astral Diary to discover your Rising Sign. This is the zodiac sign that was appearing over the Eastern horizon at the time of your birth and is just as important to you as an individual as is your Sun sign.

It is the synthesis of many different astrological possibilities that makes you what you are and with the Astral Diaries you can learn so much. How do you react to love and romance? Through the unique Venus tables and the readings that follow them, you can learn where the planet Venus was at the time of your birth. It is even possible to register when little Mercury is 'retrograde', which means that it appears to be moving backwards in space when viewed from the Earth. Mercury rules communication, so be prepared to deal with a few setbacks in this area when you see the sign ☿. The Astral Diary will be an interest and a support throughout the whole year ahead.

*Old Moore extends his customary greeting to all people of the Earth and offers his age-old wishes for a happy and prosperous period ahead.*

# THE ESSENCE OF VIRGO

*Exploring the Personality of Virgo the Virgin*

(24TH AUGUST – 24TH SEPTEMBER)

## What's in a sign?

Virgo people tend to be a rather extraordinary sort of mixture. Your ruling planet is Mercury, which makes you inclined to be rather chatty and quite sociable. On the other hand, yours is known as an Earth-ruled zodiac sign, which is usually steady and sometimes quite reserved. Thus, from the start, there are opposing energies ruling your life. This is not a problem when the right sort of balance is achieved and that is what you are looking for all the time. Repressed social and personal communication can make you worrisome, which in turn leads to a slightly fussy tendency that is not your most endearing quality.

At best you are quite ingenious and can usually rely on your strong intuition when weighing up the pros and cons of any given situation. Like all Earth signs you are able to accrue wealth and work hard to achieve your ultimate objectives in life. However, one is left with the impression that problems arise for Virgo when acquisition takes over. In other words you need to relax more and to enjoy the fruits of your successes on a more regular basis.

Tidiness is important to you, and not just around your home. You particularly don't like loose ends and can be meticulous in your sense of detail. It seems likely that the fictional Sherlock Holmes was a Virgo subject and his ability to get to the absolute root of all situations is a stock-in-trade for the sign of the Virgin. Flexibility is especially important in relationships and you shouldn't become so obsessed with the way surroundings look that you fail to make the most of social opportunities.

Another tendency for Virgo is a need to 'keep up with the Joneses'. Why do you do this? Mainly because like your fellow Mercury-ruled sign of Gemini you haven't really as much confidence as seems to be the case. As a result you want to know that you are as good as anyone else, and if possible better. This can, on occasion, lead to a sort of subconscious race that you can never hope to win. Learn to relax, and to recognise when you are on top anyway, and you are really motoring.

## Virgo resources

Virgoan people are not at all short of savvy, and one of the most important considerations about your make-up is that you usually know how to proceed in a practical sense. At your disposal you have an armoury of weapons that can lead to a successful sort of life, especially in a practical and financial sense.

Your ruling planet, Mercury, makes you a good communicator and shows you the way to get on-side with the world at large. This quality means that you are rarely short of the right sort of information that is necessary in order to get things right first time. Where this doesn't prove to be possible you have Earth-sign tenacity, and an ability to work extremely hard for long hours in order to achieve your intended objectives. On the way you tend on the whole to make friends, though you might find it hard to get through life without picking up one or two adversaries too.

Virgo people are capable of being gregarious and gossipy, whilst at the same time retaining an internal discipline which more perceptive people are inclined to recognise instinctively. You cement secure friendships and that means nearly always having someone to rely on in times of difficulty. But this isn't a one-way street, because you are a very supportive type yourself and would fight tenaciously on behalf of a person or a cause that you supported wholeheartedly. At such times you can appear to be quite brave, even though you could be quaking inside.

A tendency towards being nervy is not always as evident as you might think, mainly because you have the power and ability to keep it behind closed doors. Retaining the secrets of friends, despite your tendency to indulge in gossip, is an important part of your character and is the reason that others learn to trust you. Organisational skills are good and you love to sort out the puzzles of life, which makes you ideal for tedious jobs that many other people would find impossible to complete. Your curiosity knows no bounds and you would go to almost any length to answer questions that are uppermost in your mind at any point in time.

## Beneath the surface

So what are you really like? Well, in the case of Virgo this might be the most interesting journey of all, and one that could deeply surprise even some of those people who think they know you very well indeed. First of all it must be remembered that your ruling planet is Mercury, known as the lord of communication. As a result it's important for you to keep in touch with the world at large. That's fine, except for the fact that your Earth-sign tendencies are inclined to make you basically quiet by nature.

Here we find something of a contradiction and one that leads to more than a few misunderstandings. You are particularly sensitive to little changes out there in the cosmos and so can be much more voluble on some days than on others. The result can be that others see you as being somewhat moody, which isn't really the case at all.

You are inclined to be fairly nervy and would rarely be quite as confident as you give the impression of being. Although usually robust in terms of general health, this doesn't always seem to be the case and a tendency towards a slightly hypochondriac nature can be the result. Some Virgoans can make an art form out of believing that they are unwell and you need to understand that part of the reason for this lies in your desire for attention.

Another accusation that is levelled at Virgoans is that they are inclined to be fussy over details. This is also an expression of your lack of basic confidence in yourself. For some reason you subconsciously assume that if every last matter is dealt with absolutely, all will work out well. In reality the more relaxed you remain, the better you find your ability to cope with everyday life.

The simple truth is that you are much more capable than your inner nature tends to believe and could easily think more of yourself than you do. You have a logical mind, but also gain from the intuition that is possessed by all Mercury-ruled individuals. The more instinctive you become, the less you worry about things and the more relaxed life can seem to be. You also need to override a natural suspicion of those around you. Trust is a hard thing for you, but a very important one.

## Making the best of yourself

There are many ways in which you can exploit the best potentials of your zodiac sign, and at the same time play down some of the less favourable possibilities. From the very start it's important to realise that the main criticism that comes your way from the outside world is that you are too fussy by half. So, simply avoid being critical of others and the way they do things. By all means stick to your own opinions, but avoid forcing them onto other people. If you can get over this hurdle, your personal popularity will already be that much greater. If people love you, you care for them in return – it's as simple as that, because at heart you aren't really very complicated.

Despite the fact that a little humility would go a long way, you also do need to remain sure of yourself. There's no real problem in allowing others their head, while following your own opinions all the same. Use your practical skills to the full and don't rush things just because other people seem to do so. Although you are ruled by quick Mercury you also come from an Earth sign, which means steady progress.

Find outlets to desensitise your over-nervy nature. You can do this with plenty of healthy exercise and by taking an interest in subject matter that isn't of any great importance, but which you find appealing all the same. Avoid concentrating too much on any one thing, because that is the road to paranoia.

Realise that you have an innate sense of what is right, and that if it is utilised in the right way you can make gains for yourself and for the people you love. You have a good fund of ideas, so don't be afraid to use them. Most important of all you need to remain confident but flexible. That's the path to popularity – something you need much more than you might realise.

## The impressions you give

This can be something of a problem area to at least some people born under the zodiac sign of Virgo. There isn't much doubt that your heart is in the right place and this fact isn't lost on many observers. All the same, you can appear to be very definite in your opinions, in fact to the point of stubbornness, and you won't give ground when you know you are in the right. A slight problem here might be that Virgoans nearly always think they have the moral and legal high ground. In the majority of cases this may indeed be true, but there are ways and means of putting the message across.

What Virgo needs more than anything else is tact. A combination of Mercury, ruling your means of communication, and your Earth-sign heritage can, on occasions, make you appear to be rather blunt. Mercury also aids in quick thinking and problem solving. The sum total can make it appear that you don't take other people's opinions into account and that you are prepared to railroad your ideas through if necessary.

Most people recognise that you are very capable, and may therefore automatically turn to you for leadership. It isn't certain how you will react under any given circumstance because although you can criticise others, your Earth-sign proclivities don't make you a natural leader. In a strong supportive role you can be wonderful and it is towards this scenario that you might choose to look.

Avoid people accusing you of being fussy by deliberately cultivating flexibility in your thinking and your actions. You are one of the kindest and most capable people to be found anywhere in the zodiac. All you need to do to complete the picture is to let the world at large know what you are. With your natural kindness and your ability to get things done you can show yourself to be a really attractive individual. Look towards a brush-up of your public persona. Deep inside you are organised and caring, though a little nervy. Let people know exactly what you are – it only makes you more human.

## The way forward

Before anyone can move forward into anything it is important for them to realise exactly where they are now. In your case this is especially true. Probably the most problematic area of Virgo is in realising not what is being done but rather why. It is the inability to ask this question on a regular basis that leads Virgo into a rut now and again. Habit isn't simply a word to many people born under the zodiac sign of Virgo, it's a religion. The strange thing about this fact is that if you find yourself catapulted, against your will, into a different sort of routine, you soon learn to adopt it as if it were second nature. In other words this way of behaving is endemic, but not necessarily inevitable. The way out of it is simple and comes thanks to your ruling planet of Mercury. Keep talking, and at the same time listen. Adapt your life on a regular basis and say 'So many habits are not necessary' at least ten times a day.

All the same it wouldn't be very prudent to throw out the baby with the bath water. Your ability to stick at things is justifiably legendary. This generally means that you arrive at your desired destination in life, even though it might take you a long time to get there. The usual result is respect from people who don't have your persistence or tenacity.

With regard to love and affection you are in a good position to place a protecting blanket around those you love the most. This is fine, as long as you check regularly that you are not suffocating them with it. If you allow a certain degree of freedom people will respect your concern all the more, and they won't fight against it. By all means communicate your affection and don't allow your natural Earth-sign reserve to get in the way of expressing feelings that are quite definite internally. This is another aspect of letting the world know what you are really like and is of crucial importance to your zodiac sign.

You need variety, and if possible an absence of worry. Only when things are going wrong do Virgoans become the fussy individuals that sometimes attract a little criticism. As long as you feel that you are in charge of your own destiny, you can remain optimistic – another vital requisite for Virgo. With just a little effort you can be one of the most popular and loved people around. Add to this your natural ability to succeed and the prognosis for the sign of the Virgin is very good.

# VIRGO ON THE CUSP

Old Moore is often asked how astrological profiles are altered for those people born at either the beginning or the end of a zodiac sign, or, more properly, on the cusps of a sign. In the case of Virgo this would be on the 24th of August and for two or three days after, and similarly at the end of the sign, probably from the 21st to the 23rd of September. In this year's Astral Diaries, once again, Old Moore sets out to explain the differences regarding cuspid signs.

## The Leo Cusp – August 24th to 26th

If anything is designed to lighten the load of being a Virgoan, it's having a Leo quality in the nature too. All Virgoans are inclined to take themselves too seriously on occasions and they don't have half as much self-esteem as they could really use effectively. Being born on the Leo cusp gives better self-confidence, less of the supreme depths which Virgo alone can display and a much more superficial view of many aspects of life. The material success for which Virgo is famous probably won't be lacking, but there will also be a determination to have fun and let the bright, aspiring qualities that are so popular in the Leo character show.

In matters of love, you are likely to be easy-going, bright, bubbly and always willing to have a laugh. You relish good company, and though you sometimes go at things like a bull at a gate, your intentions are true and you know how to get others to like you a great deal. Family matters are right up your street, because not only do you have the ability to put down firm and enduring roots, but you are the most staunch and loyal protector of family values that anyone could wish for.

When it comes to working, you seem to have the best combination of all. You have the ability to work long and hard, achieving your objectives as all Virgoans do, but managing to do so with a smile permanently fixed to your face. You are naturally likely to find yourself at the head of things, where your combination of skills is going to be of the greatest use. This sign combination is to be found in every nook and cranny of the working world but perhaps less frequently in jobs which involve getting your hands dirty.

There are times when you definitely live on your nerves and when you don't get the genuine relaxation that the Virgoan qualities within you demand. Chances are you are much more robust than you consider yourself to be, and as long as you keep busy most of the time you tend to enjoy a contented life. The balance usually works well, because Leo lifts Virgo, whilst Virgo stabilises an often too superficial Lion.

## The Libra Cusp – September 21st to 23rd

Virgo responds well to input from other parts of the zodiac and probably never more so than in the case of the Libran cusp. The reasons for this are very simple: what Virgo on its own lacks, Libra possesses, and it's the same on the other side of the coin. Libra is often flighty and doesn't take enough time to rest, but it is compensated by the balance inherent in the sign, so it weighs things carefully. Virgo on the other hand is deep and sometimes dark, but because it's ruled by capricious little Mercury, it can also be rather too impetuous. The potential break-even point is obvious and usually leads to a fairly easy-going individual, who is intellectual, thoughtful and practical when necessary.

You are a great person to have around in good times and bad, and you know how to have fun. A staunch support and helper to your friends, you enjoy a high degree of popularity, which usually extends to affairs of the heart. There may be more than one of these in your life and it's best for people born on this cusp not to marry in haste or too early in life. But even if you get things wrong first time around, you have the ability to bounce back quickly and don't become easily discouraged. It is good for you to be often in the company of gregarious and interesting people, but you are quite capable of surviving on your own when you have to.

Health matters may be on your mind more than is strictly necessary, and it's true that you can sometimes worry yourself into minor ailments that would not otherwise have existed. It is important for you to get plenty of rest and also to enjoy yourself. The more you work on behalf of others, the less time you spend thinking about your own possible ailments. Anxiety needs to be avoided, often by getting to the root of a problem and solving it quickly.

A capable and committed worker, you are at your best when able to share the decisions, but you are quite reliable when you have to make up your mind alone. You would never bully those beneath you. You are never short of support and you bring joy to life most of the time.

# VIRGO AND ITS ASCENDANTS

The nature of every individual on the planet is composed of the rich variety of zodiac signs and planetary positions that were present at the time of their birth. Your Sun sign, which in your case is Virgo, is one of the many factors when it comes to assessing the unique person you are. Probably the most important consideration, other than your Sun sign, is to establish the zodiac sign that was rising over the eastern horizon at the time that you were born. This is your Ascending or Rising sign. Most popular astrology fails to take account of the Ascendant, and yet its importance remains with you from the very moment of your birth, through every day of your life. The Ascendant is evident in the way you approach the world, and so, when meeting a person for the first time, it is this astrological influence that you are most likely to notice first. Our Ascending sign essentially represents what we appear to be, while the Sun sign is what we feel inside ourselves.

The Ascendant also has the potential for modifying our overall nature. For example, if you were born at a time of day when Virgo was passing over the eastern horizon (this would be around the time of dawn) then you would be classed as a double Virgo. As such, you would typify this zodiac sign, both internally and in your dealings with others. However, if your Ascendant sign turned out to be a Fire sign, such as Aries, there would be a profound alteration of nature, away from the expected qualities of Virgo.

One of the reasons why popular astrology often ignores the Ascendant is that it has always been rather difficult to establish. Old Moore has found a way to make this possible by devising an easy-to-use table, which you will find on page 125 of this book. Using this, you can establish your Ascendant sign at a glance. You will need to know your rough time of birth, then it is simply a case of following the instructions.

For those readers who have no idea of their time of birth it might be worth allowing a good friend, or perhaps your partner, to read through the section that follows this introduction. Someone who deals with you on a regular basis may easily discover your Ascending sign, even though you could have some difficulty establishing it for yourself. A good understanding of this component of your nature is essential if you want to be aware of that 'other person' who is responsible for the way you make contact with the world at large. Your Sun sign, Ascendant sign, and the other pointers in this book will, together, allow you a far better understanding of what makes you tick as an individual. Peeling back the different layers of your astrological make-up can be an enlightening experience, and the Ascendant may represent one of the most important layers of all.

## Virgo with Virgo Ascendant

You get the best of both worlds, and on rare occasions the worst too. Frighteningly efficient, you have the ability to scare people with your constant knack of getting it right. This won't endear you to everyone, particularly those who pride themselves on being disorganised. You make a loyal friend and would do almost anything for someone who is important to you, though you do so in a quiet way because you are not the most noisy of types. Chances are that you possess the ability to write well and you also have a cultured means of verbal communication on those occasions when you really choose to speak out.

It isn't difficult for you to argue your case, though much of the time you refuse to do so and can lock yourself into your own private world for days on end. If you are at ease with yourself you possess a powerful personality, which you can express well. Conversely, you can live on your nerves and cause problems for yourself. Meditation is good, fussing over details that really don't matter at all is less useful. Once you have chosen a particular course of action there are few people around with sufficient will-power to prevent you from getting what you want. Wide open spaces where the hand of nature is all around can make you feel very relaxed.

## Virgo with Libra Ascendant

Libra has the ability to lighten almost any load and it is particularly good at doing so when it is brought together with the much more repressed sign of Virgo. To the world at large you seem relaxed, happy and able to cope with most of the pressures that life places upon you. Not only do you deal with your own life in a bright and breezy manner but you are usually on hand to help others out of any dilemma that they might make for themselves. With excellent powers of communication you leave the world at large in no doubt whatsoever concerning both your opinions and your wishes. It is in the talking stakes that you really excel because Virgo brings the silver tongue of Mercury and Libra adds the Air-sign desire to be in constant touch with the world outside your door.

You like to have a good time and are often found in the company of interesting and stimulating people, who have the ability to bring out the very best in your bright and sparkling personality. Underneath however, there is still much of the worrying Virgoan to be found and this means that you have to learn to relax inside as well as appearing to do so externally. In fact you are much more complex than most people would realise and definitely would not be suited to a life that allowed you too much time to think about yourself.

## Virgo with Scorpio Ascendant

This is intensity carried through to the absolute. If you have a problem it is that you fail to externalise all that is going on inside that deep, bubbling cauldron of your inner self. Realising what you are capable of is not a problem, these only start when you have to make it plain to those around you what you want. Part of the reason for this is that you don't always understand yourself. You love intensely and would do absolutely anything for a person you are fond of, even though you might have to inconvenience yourself a great deal on the way. Relationships can cause you slight problems however, since you need to associate with people who at least come somewhere near to understanding what makes you tick. If you manage to bridge the gap between yourself and the world that constantly knocks on your door, you show yourself to be powerful, magnetic and compulsive.

There are times when you definitely prefer to stay quiet though you do have a powerful ability to get your message across when you think it is necessary to do so. There are people around who might think that you are a push-over but they could easily get a shock when you sense that the time is right to answer back. You probably have a very orderly house and don't care for clutter of any sort.

## Virgo with Sagittarius Ascendant

This is a combination that might look rather odd at first sight because these two signs have so very little in common. However the saying goes that opposites attract and in terms of the personality you display to the world this is especially true in your case. Not everyone understands what makes you tick but you try to show the least complicated face to the world that you can manage to display. You can be deep and secretive on occasions, and yet at other times you can start talking as soon as you climb out of bed and never stop until you are back there again. Inspirational and spontaneous, you take the world by storm on those occasions when you are free from worries and firing on all cylinders. It is a fact that you support your friends, though there are rather more of them than would be the case for Virgo taken on its own and you don't always choose them as wisely as you might.

There are times when you display a temper and although Sagittarius is incapable of bearing a grudge, the same cannot be said for Virgo, which has a better memory than the elephant. For the best results in life you need to relax as much as possible and avoid overheating that powerful and busy brain. Virgo gives you the ability to concentrate on one thing at once, a skill you should encourage.

## Virgo with Capricorn Ascendant

Your endurance, persistence and concentration are legendary and there is virtually nothing that eludes you once you have the bit between your teeth. You are not the pushy, fussy, go-getting sort of Virgoan but are steady, methodical and very careful. Once you have made up your mind, a whole team of wild horses could not change it and although this can be a distinct blessing at times, it is a quality that can bring odd problems into your life too. The difficulty starts when you adopt a lost or less than sensible cause. Even in the face of overwhelming evidence that you are wrong there is something inside you that prevents any sort of U-turn and so you walk forward as solidly as only you are able, to a destination that won't suit you at all.

There are few people around who are more loyal and constant than you can be. There is a lighter and brighter side to your nature and the one or two people who are most important in your life will know how to bring it out. You have a wicked sense of humour, particularly if you have had a drink or when you are feeling on top form. Travel does you the world of good, even if there is a part of you that would rather stay at home. You have a potent, powerful and magnetic personality but for much of the time it is kept carefully hidden.

## Virgo with Aquarius Ascendant

How could anyone make convention unconventional? Well, if anyone can manage, you can. There are great contradictions here because on the one hand you always want to do what is expected, but the Aquarian quality within your nature loves to surprise everyone on the way. If you don't always know what you are thinking or doing, it's a pretty safe bet that others won't either, so it's important on occasions to stop and really think. However this is not a pressing concern because you tend to live a fairly happy life and muddle through no matter what. Other people tend to take to you well and it is likely that you will have many friends. You tend to be bright and cheerful and can approach even difficult tasks with the certainty that you have the skills necessary to see them through to their conclusion. Give and take are important factors in the life of any individual and particularly so in your case. Because you can stretch yourself in order to understand what makes other people think and act in the way that they do, you have the reputation of being a good friend and a reliable colleague.

In love you can be somewhat more fickle than the typical Virgoan and yet you are always interesting to live with. Where you are, things happen, and you mix a sparkling wit with deep insights.

## Virgo with Pisces Ascendant

You might have been accused on occasions of being too sensitive for your own good, a charge that is not entirely without foundation. Certainly you are very understanding of the needs of others, sometimes to the extent that you put everything aside to help them. This would also be true in the case of charities, for you care very much about the world and the people who cling tenaciously to its surface. Your ability to love on a one-to-one basis knows no bounds though you may not discriminate as much as you could, particularly when young, and might have one or two false starts in the love stakes. You don't always choose to verbalise your thoughts and this can cause problems, because there is always so much going on in your mind and Virgo especially needs good powers of communication. Pisces is quieter and you need to force yourself to say what you think when the explanation is important.

You would never betray a confidence and sometimes take on rather more for the sake of your friends than is strictly good for you. This is not a fault but can cause you problems all the same. Because you are so intuitive there is little that escapes your attention, though you should avoid being pessimistic about your insights. Changes of scenery suit you and extensive travel would bring out the best in what can be a repressed nature at times.

## Virgo with Aries Ascendant

Virgo is steady and sure, though also fussy and stubborn. Aries is fast and determined, restless and active. It can be seen already that this is a rather strange meeting of characteristics and because Virgo is ruled by capricious Mercury, the result will change from hour to hour and day to day. It isn't merely that others find it difficult to know where they are with you; they can't even understand what makes you tick. This will make you the subject of endless fascination and attention, at which you will be apparently surprised but inwardly pleased. If anyone ever really gets to know what goes on in that busy mind they may find the implications very difficult to deal with and it is a fact that only you would have the ability to live inside your crowded head.

As a partner and a parent you are second to none, though you would tend to get on better with your children once they started to grow, since by this time you may be slightly less restricting to their own desires, which will often clash with your own on their behalf. You are capable of give and take and could certainly not be considered selfish, though your desire to get the best from everyone might be misconstrued on occasion.

## Virgo with Taurus Ascendant

This combination tends to amplify the Taurean qualities that you naturally possess and this is the case because both Taurus and Virgo are Earth signs. However, there are certain factors related to Virgo that show themselves very differently than the sign's cousin Taurus. Virgo is more fussy, nervy and pedantic than Taurus and all of these qualities are going to show up in your nature at one level or another. On the plus side you might be slightly less concerned about having a perfect home and a perfect family, and your interest in life appears at a more direct level than that of the true Taurean. You care very much about your home and family and are very loyal to your friends. It's true that you sometimes tend to try and take them over and you can also show a marked tendency to dominate, but your heart is in the right place and most people recognise that your caring is genuine.

One problem is that there are very few shades of grey in your life, which is certainly not the case for other zodiac sign combinations. Living your life in the way that you do there isn't much room for compromise and this fact alone can prove to be something of a problem where relationships are concerned. In a personal sense you need a partner who is willing to be organised and one who relies on your judgements, which don't change all that often.

## Virgo with Gemini Ascendant

A Gemini Ascendant means that you are ruled by Mercury, both through your Sun sign and through the sign that was rising at the time of your birth. This means that words are your basic tools in life and you use them to the full. Some writers have this combination, because even speaking to people virtually all the time is not enough. Although you have many friends you are fairly high-minded, which means that you can make enemies too. The fact is that people either care very much for you, or else they don't like you at all. This can be difficult for you to come to terms with because you don't really set out to cause friction – it simply attracts itself to you.

Although you love travel, home is important too and there is a basic insecurity in your nature that comes about as a result of an overdose of Mercury, which makes you nervy and sometimes far less confident than anyone would guess. Success in your life may be slower arriving with this combination because you are determined to achieve your objectives on your own terms and this can take time. Always a contradiction, often a puzzle to others, your ultimate happiness in life is directly proportional to the effort you put in, though this should not mean wearing yourself out on the way.

## Virgo with Cancer Ascendant

What can this union of zodiac signs bring to the party that isn't there in either Virgo or Cancer alone? Well quite a bit actually. Virgo can be very fussy on occasions and too careful for its own good. The presence of steady, serene Cancer alters the perspectives and allows a smoother, more flowing Virgoan to greet the world. You are chatty, easy to know and exhibit a combination of the practical skills of Virgo, together with the deep and penetrating insights that are typical of Cancer. This can make you appear to be very powerful, and your insights are second to none. You are a born organiser and love to be where things are happening, even if you are only there to help make the sandwiches or to pour the tea. Invariably your role will be much greater but you don't seek personal acclaim and are a good team player on most occasions.

There is a quiet side to your nature and those who live with you will eventually get used to your need for solitude. This seems strange because Virgo is generally such a chatterbox and, taken on its own, is rarely quiet for long. In love you show great affection and a sense of responsibility that makes you an ideal parent, though it is possible sometimes that you care rather more than you are willing to show.

## Virgo with Leo Ascendant

Here we have cheerfulness allied to efficiency, which can be a very positive combination most of the time. With all the sense of honour, justice and bravery of the Leo subject, Virgo adds staying power through tedious situations and offers you a slightly more serious view of life than we would expect from the Lion alone. In almost any situation you can keep going until you get to your chosen destination and you also find the time to reach out to the people who need your unique nature the most. Few would deny your kindness, though you can attract a little envy because it seems as though yours is the sort of personality that everyone else wants.

Most people born with this combination have a radiant smile and will do their best to think situations through carefully. If there is a tendency to be foolhardy, it is carefully masked beneath a covering of Virgoan common sense. Family matters are dealt with efficiently and with great love. Some might see you as close one moment and distant the next. The truth is that you are always on the go and have a thousand different things to think about, all at the same time. On the whole your presence is noticed and you may represent the most loyal friend of them all.

# THE MOON AND THE PART IT PLAYS IN YOUR LIFE

In astrology the Moon is probably the single most important heavenly body after the Sun. Its unique position, as partner to the Earth on its journey around the solar system, means that the Moon appears to pass through the signs of the zodiac extremely quickly. The zodiac position of the Moon at the time of your birth plays a great part in personal character and is especially significant in the build-up of your emotional nature.

## Sun Moon Cycles

The first lunar cycle deals with the part the position of the Moon plays relative to your Sun sign. I have made the fluctuations of this pattern easy for you to understand by means of a simple cyclic graph. It appears on the first page of each 'Your Month At A Glance', under the title 'Highs and Lows'. The graph displays the lunar cycle and you will soon learn to understand how its movements have a bearing on your level of energy and your abilities.

## Your Own Moon Sign

Discovering the position of the Moon at the time of your birth has always been notoriously difficult because tracking the complex zodiac positions of the Moon is not easy. This process has been reduced to three simple stages with Old Moore's unique Lunar Tables. A breakdown of the Moon's zodiac positions can be found from page 28 onwards, so that once you know what your Moon Sign is, you can see what part this plays in the overall build-up of your personal character.

If you follow the instructions on the next page you will soon be able to work out exactly what zodiac sign the Moon occupied on the day that you were born and you can then go on to compare the reading for this position with those of your Sun sign and your Ascendant. It is partly the comparison between these three important positions that goes towards making you the unique individual you are.

# HOW TO DISCOVER YOUR MOON SIGN

This is a three-stage process. You may need a pen and a piece of paper but if you follow the instructions below the process should only take a minute or so.

**STAGE 1** First of all you need to know the Moon Age at the time of your birth. If you look at Moon Table 1, on page 26, you will find all the years between 1917 and 2015 down the left side. Find the year of your birth and then trace across to the right to the month of your birth. Where the two intersect you will find a number. This is the date of the New Moon in the month that you were born. You now need to count forward the number of days between the New Moon and your own birthday. For example, if the New Moon in the month of your birth was shown as being the 6th and you were born on the 20th, your Moon Age Day would be 14. If the New Moon in the month of your birth came after your birthday, you need to count forward from the New Moon in the previous month. If you were born in a Leap Year, remember to count the 29th February. You can tell if your birth year was a Leap Year if the last two digits can be divided by four. Whatever the result, jot this number down so that you do not forget it.

**STAGE 2** Take a look at Moon Table 2 on page 27. Down the left hand column look for the date of your birth. Now trace across to the month of your birth. Where the two meet you will find a letter. Copy this letter down alongside your Moon Age Day.

**STAGE 3** Moon Table 3 on page 27 will supply you with the zodiac sign the Moon occupied on the day of your birth. Look for your Moon Age Day down the left hand column and then for the letter you found in Stage 2. Where the two converge you will find a zodiac sign and this is the sign occupied by the Moon on the day that you were born.

## Your Zodiac Moon Sign Explained

You will find a profile of all zodiac Moon Signs on pages 28 to 31, showing in yet another way how astrology helps to make you into the individual that you are. In each daily entry of the Astral Diary you can find the zodiac position of the Moon for every day of the year. This also allows you to discover your lunar birthdays. Since the Moon passes through all the signs of the zodiac in about a month, you can expect something like twelve lunar birthdays each year. At these times you are likely to be emotionally steady and able to make the sort of decisions that have real, lasting value.

# Moon Table I

| YEAR | JUL | AUG | SEP | YEAR | JUL | AUG | SEP | YEAR | JUL | AUG | SEP |
|---|---|---|---|---|---|---|---|---|---|---|---|
| 1917 | 18 | 17 | 15 | 1950 | 15 | 13 | 12 | 1983 | 10 | 8 | 7 |
| 1918 | 8 | 6 | 4 | 1951 | 4 | 2 | 1 | 1984 | 28 | 26 | 25 |
| 1919 | 27 | 25 | 23 | 1952 | 23 | 20 | 19 | 1985 | 17 | 16 | 14 |
| 1920 | 15 | 14 | 12 | 1953 | 11 | 9 | 8 | 1986 | 7 | 5 | 4 |
| 1921 | 5 | 3 | 2 | 1954 | 29 | 28 | 27 | 1987 | 25 | 24 | 23 |
| 1922 | 24 | 22 | 21 | 1955 | 19 | 17 | 16 | 1988 | 13 | 12 | 11 |
| 1923 | 14 | 12 | 10 | 1956 | 8 | 6 | 4 | 1989 | 3 | 1/31 | 29 |
| 1924 | 2/31 | 30 | 28 | 1957 | 27 | 25 | 23 | 1990 | 22 | 20 | 19 |
| 1925 | 20 | 19 | 18 | 1958 | 16 | 15 | 13 | 1991 | 11 | 9 | 8 |
| 1926 | 9 | 8 | 7 | 1959 | 6 | 4 | 3 | 1992 | 29 | 28 | 26 |
| 1927 | 28 | 27 | 25 | 1960 | 24 | 22 | 21 | 1993 | 19 | 17 | 16 |
| 1928 | 17 | 16 | 14 | 1961 | 12 | 11 | 10 | 1994 | 8 | 7 | 5 |
| 1929 | 6 | 5 | 3 | 1962 | 1/31 | 30 | 28 | 1995 | 27 | 26 | 24 |
| 1930 | 25 | 24 | 22 | 1963 | 20 | 19 | 17 | 1996 | 15 | 14 | 13 |
| 1931 | 15 | 13 | 12 | 1964 | 9 | 7 | 6 | 1997 | 4 | 3 | 2 |
| 1932 | 3 | 2/31 | 30 | 1965 | 28 | 26 | 25 | 1998 | 23 | 22 | 20 |
| 1933 | 22 | 21 | 19 | 1966 | 17 | 16 | 14 | 1999 | 13 | 11 | 10 |
| 1934 | 11 | 10 | 9 | 1967 | 7 | 5 | 4 | 2000 | 1/31 | 29 | 27 |
| 1935 | 30 | 29 | 27 | 1968 | 25 | 24 | 23 | 2001 | 20 | 19 | 17 |
| 1936 | 18 | 17 | 15 | 1969 | 13 | 12 | 11 | 2002 | 9 | 8 | 6 |
| 1937 | 8 | 6 | 4 | 1970 | 4 | 2 | 1 | 2003 | 28 | 27 | 26 |
| 1938 | 27 | 25 | 23 | 1971 | 22 | 20 | 19 | 2004 | 16 | 14 | 13 |
| 1939 | 16 | 15 | 13 | 1972 | 11 | 9 | 8 | 2005 | 6 | 4 | 3 |
| 1940 | 5 | 4 | 2 | 1973 | 29 | 28 | 27 | 2006 | 25 | 23 | 22 |
| 1941 | 24 | 22 | 21 | 1974 | 19 | 17 | 16 | 2007 | 15 | 13 | 12 |
| 1942 | 13 | 12 | 10 | 1975 | 9 | 7 | 5 | 2008 | 31 | 31 | 30 |
| 1943 | 2 | 1/30 | 29 | 1976 | 27 | 25 | 23 | 2009 | 22 | 20 | 19 |
| 1944 | 20 | 18 | 17 | 1977 | 16 | 14 | 13 | 2010 | 12 | 10 | 8 |
| 1945 | 9 | 8 | 6 | 1978 | 5 | 4 | 2 | 2011 | 2/31 | 29 | 27 |
| 1946 | 28 | 26 | 25 | 1979 | 24 | 22 | 21 | 2012 | 19 | 17 | 16 |
| 1947 | 17 | 16 | 14 | 1980 | 12 | 11 | 10 | 2013 | 7 | 6 | 4 |
| 1948 | 6 | 5 | 3 | 1981 | 1/31 | 29 | 28 | 2014 | 25 | 24 | 23 |
| 1949 | 25 | 24 | 23 | 1982 | 20 | 19 | 17 | 2015 | 16 | 15 | 13 |

## Table 2

| DAY | AUG | SEP |
|---|---|---|
| 1 | U | X |
| 2 | U | X |
| 3 | V | X |
| 4 | V | Y |
| 5 | V | Y |
| 6 | V | Y |
| 7 | V | Y |
| 8 | V | Y |
| 9 | V | Y |
| 10 | V | Y |
| 11 | V | Y |
| 12 | V | Y |
| 13 | V | Y |
| 14 | W | Z |
| 15 | W | Z |
| 16 | W | Z |
| 17 | W | Z |
| 18 | W | Z |
| 19 | W | Z |
| 20 | W | Z |
| 21 | W | Z |
| 22 | W | Z |
| 23 | W | Z |
| 24 | X | a |
| 25 | X | a |
| 26 | X | a |
| 27 | X | a |
| 28 | X | a |
| 29 | X | a |
| 30 | X | a |
| 31 | X | – |

## Table 3

| M/D | U | V | W | X | Y | Z | a |
|---|---|---|---|---|---|---|---|
| 0 | LE | LE | LE | VI | VI | LI | LI |
| 1 | LE | VI | VI | VI | LI | LI | LI |
| 2 | VI | VI | VI | LI | LI | LI | LI |
| 3 | VI | VI | LI | LI | LI | SC | SC |
| 4 | LI | LI | LI | LI | SC | SC | SC |
| 5 | LI | LI | SC | SC | SC | SC | SA |
| 6 | LI | SC | SC | SC | SA | SA | SA |
| 7 | SC | SC | SA | SA | SA | SA | SA |
| 8 | SC | SC | SA | SA | SA | CP | CP |
| 9 | SA | SA | SA | SA | CP | CP | CP |
| 10 | SA | SA | CP | CP | CP | CP | AQ |
| 11 | CP | CP | CP | CP | AQ | AQ | AQ |
| 12 | CP | CP | AQ | AQ | AQ | AQ | PI |
| 13 | CP | CP | AQ | AQ | AQ | PI | PI |
| 14 | AQ | AQ | PI | PI | PI | PI | AR |
| 15 | AQ | AQ | PI | PI | PI | PI | AR |
| 16 | AQ | PI | PI | PI | AR | AR | AR |
| 17 | PI | PI | PI | AR | AR | AR | AR |
| 18 | PI | PI | AR | AR | AR | AR | TA |
| 19 | PI | AR | AR | AR | TA | TA | TA |
| 20 | AR | AR | TA | TA | TA | TA | GE |
| 21 | AR | TA | TA | TA | GE | GE | GE |
| 22 | TA | TA | TA | GE | GE | GE | GE |
| 23 | TA | TA | GE | GE | GE | GE | CA |
| 24 | TA | GE | GE | GE | CA | CA | CA |
| 25 | GE | GE | CA | CA | CA | CA | CA |
| 26 | GE | CA | CA | CA | LE | LE | LE |
| 27 | CA | CA | CA | LE | LE | LE | LE |
| 28 | CA | CA | LE | LE | LE | LE | VI |
| 29 | CA | LE | LE | LE | VI | VI | VI |

AR = Aries, TA = Taurus, GE = Gemini, CA = Cancer, LE = Leo, VI = Virgo, LI = Libra, SC = Scorpio, SA = Sagittarius, CP = Capricorn, AQ = Aquarius, PI = Pisces

# MOON SIGNS

## Moon in Aries

You have a strong imagination, courage, determination and a desire to do things in your own way and forge your own path through life.

Originality is a key attribute; you are seldom stuck for ideas although your mind is changeable and you could take the time to focus on individual tasks. Often quick-tempered, you take orders from few people and live life at a fast pace. Avoid health problems by taking regular time out for rest and relaxation.

Emotionally, it is important that you talk to those you are closest to and work out your true feelings. Once you discover that people are there to help, there is less necessity for you to do everything yourself.

## Moon in Taurus

The Moon in Taurus gives you a courteous and friendly manner, which means you are likely to have many friends.

The good things in life mean a lot to you, as Taurus is an Earth sign that delights in experiences which please the senses. Hence you are probably a lover of good food and drink, which may in turn mean you need to keep an eye on the bathroom scales, especially as looking good is also important to you.

Emotionally you are fairly stable and you stick by your own standards. Taureans do not respond well to change. Intuition also plays an important part in your life.

## Moon in Gemini

You have a warm-hearted character, sympathetic and eager to help others. At times reserved, you can also be articulate and chatty: this is part of the paradox of Gemini, which always brings duplicity to the nature. You are interested in current affairs, have a good intellect, and are good company and likely to have many friends. Most of your friends have a high opinion of you and would be ready to defend you should the need arise. However, this is usually unnecessary, as you are quite capable of defending yourself in any verbal confrontation.

Travel is important to your inquisitive mind and you find intellectual stimulus in mixing with people from different cultures. You also gain much from reading, writing and the arts but you do need plenty of rest and relaxation in order to avoid fatigue.

## Moon in Cancer

The Moon in Cancer at the time of birth is a fortunate position as Cancer is the Moon's natural home. This means that the qualities of compassion and understanding given by the Moon are especially enhanced in your nature, and you are friendly and sociable and cope well with emotional pressures. You cherish home and family life, and happily do the domestic tasks. Your surroundings are important to you and you hate squalor and filth. You are likely to have a love of music and poetry.

Your basic character, although at times changeable like the Moon itself, depends on symmetry. You aim to make your surroundings comfortable and harmonious, for yourself and those close to you.

## Moon in Leo

The best qualities of the Moon and Leo come together to make you warmhearted, fair, ambitious and self-confident. With good organisational abilities, you invariably rise to a position of responsibility in your chosen career. This is fortunate as you don't enjoy being an 'also-ran' and would rather be an important part of a small organisation than a menial in a large one.

You should be lucky in love, and happy, provided you put in the effort to make a comfortable home for yourself and those close to you. It is likely that you will have a love of pleasure, sport, music and literature. Life brings you many rewards, most of them as a direct result of your own efforts, although you may be luckier than average and ready to make the best of any situation.

## Moon in Virgo

You are endowed with good mental abilities and a keen receptive memory, but you are never ostentatious or pretentious. Naturally quite reserved, you still have many friends, especially of the opposite sex. Marital relationships must be discussed carefully and worked at so that they remain harmonious, as personal attachments can be a problem if you do not give them your full attention.

Talented and persevering, you possess artistic qualities and are a good homemaker. Earning your honours through genuine merit, you work long and hard towards your objectives but show little pride in your achievements. Many short journeys will be undertaken in your life.

## Moon in Libra

With the Moon in Libra you are naturally popular and make friends easily. People like you, probably more than you realise, you bring fun to a party and are a natural diplomat. For all its good points, Libra is not the most stable of astrological signs and, as a result, your emotions can be a little unstable too. Therefore, although the Moon in Libra is said to be good for love and marriage, your Sun sign and Rising sign will have an important effect on your emotional and loving qualities.

You must remember to relate to others in your decision-making. Co-operation is crucial because Libra represents the 'balance' of life that can only be achieved through harmonious relationships. Conformity is not easy for you because Libra, an Air sign, likes its independence.

## Moon in Scorpio

Some people might call you pushy. In fact, all you really want to do is to live life to the full and protect yourself and your family from the pressures of life. Take care to avoid giving the impression of being sarcastic or impulsive and use your energies wisely and constructively.

You have great courage and you invariably achieve your goals by force of personality and sheer effort. You are fond of mystery and are good at predicting the outcome of situations and events. Travel experiences can be beneficial to you.

You may experience problems if you do not take time to examine your motives in a relationship, and also if you allow jealousy, always a feature of Scorpio, to cloud your judgement.

## Moon in Sagittarius

The Moon in Sagittarius helps to make you a generous individual with humanitarian qualities and a kind heart. Restlessness may be intrinsic as your mind is seldom still. Perhaps because of this, you have a need for change that could lead you to several major moves during your adult life. You are not afraid to stand your ground when you know your judgement is right, you speak directly and have good intuition.

At work you are quick, efficient and versatile and so you make an ideal employee. You need work to be intellectually demanding and do not enjoy tedious routines.

In relationships, you anger quickly if faced with stupidity or deception, though you are just as quick to forgive and forget. Emotionally, there are times when your heart rules your head.

## Moon in Capricorn

The Moon in Capricorn makes you popular and likely to come into the public eye in some way. The watery Moon is not entirely comfortable in the Earth sign of Capricorn and this may lead to some difficulties in the early years of life. An initial lack of creative ability and indecision must be overcome before the true qualities of patience and perseverance inherent in Capricorn can show through.

You have good administrative ability and are a capable worker, and if you are careful you can accumulate wealth. But you must be cautious and take professional advice in partnerships, as you are open to deception. You may be interested in social or welfare work, which suit your organisational skills and sympathy for others.

## Moon in Aquarius

The Moon in Aquarius makes you an active and agreeable person with a friendly, easy-going nature. Sympathetic to the needs of others, you flourish in a laid-back atmosphere. You are broad-minded, fair and open to suggestion, although sometimes you have an unconventional quality which others can find hard to understand.

You are interested in the strange and curious, and in old articles and places. You enjoy trips to these places and gain much from them. Political, scientific and educational work interests you and you might choose a career in science or technology.

Money-wise, you make gains through innovation and concentration and Lunar Aquarians often tackle more than one job at a time. In love you are kind and honest.

## Moon in Pisces

You have a kind, sympathetic nature, somewhat retiring at times, but you always take account of others' feelings and help when you can.

Personal relationships may be problematic, but as life goes on you can learn from your experiences and develop a better understanding of yourself and the world around you.

You have a fondness for travel, appreciate beauty and harmony and hate disorder and strife. You may be fond of literature and would make a good writer or speaker yourself. You have a creative imagination and may come across as an incurable romantic. You have strong intuition, maybe bordering on a mediumistic quality, which sets you apart from the mass. You may not be rich in cash terms, but your personal gifts are worth more than gold.

# VIRGO IN LOVE

Discover how compatible you are with people from the same and other signs of the zodiac. Five stars equals a match made in heaven!

## Virgo meets Virgo

Unlike many same-sign combinations this is not a five-star pairing, for one very good reason. Virgo needs to react with other signs to reveal its hidden best side. Two Virgoans together, although enjoying some happiness, will not present a dynamic, sparkling and carefree appearance. They should run an efficient and financially sound household, but that all-important ingredient, passion, may be distinctly low-key. Star rating: ***

## Virgo meets Libra

There have been some rare occasions when this match has found great success, but usually the inward-looking Virgoan depresses the naturally gregarious Libran. Libra appears self-confident but is not so beneath the surface and needs encouragement to develop inner confidence, which may not come from Virgo. Constancy can be a problem for Libra, who also tires easily and may find Virgo dull. A less serious approach from Virgo is needed to make this work. Star rating: **

## Virgo meets Scorpio

There are one or two potential difficulties here, but there is also a meeting point from which to overcome them. Virgo is very caring and protective, a trait which Scorpio understands and even emulates. Both signs are consistent, but also sarcastic. Scorpio will impress Virgo with its serious side, and may also uncover a hidden passion in Virgo which all too often lies deep within its Earth-sign nature. Material success is very likely, with Virgo taking the lion's share of domestic chores and family responsibilities. Star rating: ***

## Virgo meets Sagittarius

There can be some strange happenings in this relationship. Sagittarius and Virgo view life so differently there are always new discoveries. Virgo is much more of a home bird than Sagittarius, but that won't matter if the Archer introduces its hectic social life gradually. More importantly, Sagittarius understands that it takes Virgo a long time to free its hidden 'inner sprite', but once free it will be fun all the way – until Virgo's thrifty nature takes over. There are great possibilities, but effort is required. Star rating: ***

## Virgo meets Capricorn

One of the best possible combinations, because Virgo and Capricorn have an instinctive understanding. Both signs know the value of dedicated hard work and apply it equally in a relationship and other areas of life. Two of the most practical signs, nothing is beyond their ken, even if to outsiders they appear rather sterile or lacking in 'oomph'. What matters most is that the individuals are happy, and with so much in common, the likelihood of mutual material success and a shared devotion to home and family, there isn't much doubt of that. Star rating: *****

## Virgo meets Aquarius

Aquarius is a strange sign because no matter how well one knows it, it always manages to surprise, and for this reason, against the odds, it's quite likely that Aquarius will form a successful relationship with Virgo. Aquarius is changeable, unpredictable and often quite 'odd' while Virgo is steady, a fuss-pot and very practical. Herein lies the key. What one sign needs, the other provides and that may be the surest recipe for success imaginable. On-lookers may not know why the couple are happy, but they will recognise that this is the case. Star rating: ****

## Virgo meets Pisces

This looks an unpromising match from beginning to end. There are exceptions to every rule, particularly where Pisces is concerned, but these two signs are both so deep it's hard to imagine that they could ever find what makes the other tick. Virgo's ruminations are extremely materialistic, while Pisces exists in a world of deep-felt, poorly expressed emotion. Pisces and Virgo might find they don't talk much, so only in a contemplative, almost monastic, match would they ever get on. Still, in a vast zodiac, anything is possible. Star rating: **

## Virgo meets Aries

Neither of these signs really understands the other, and that could easily lead to a clash. Virgo is so pedantic, which will drive Aries up the wall, while Aries always wants to be moving on to the next objective before Virgo is even settled with the last one. It will take time for these two to get to know each other, but this is a great business matching. If a personal relationship is seen in these terms then the prognosis can be quite good, but on the whole, this is not an inspiring match. Star rating: ***

## Virgo meets Taurus

This is a difficult basis for a successful relationship, and yet it often works. Both signs are from the Earth element, so have a common-sense approach to life. They have a mutual understanding, and share many interests. Taurus understands and copes well with Virgo's fussy nature, while Virgo revels in the Bull's tidy and artistic qualities. Both sides are committed to achieving lasting material success. There won't be fireworks, and the match may lack a certain 'spiritual' feel, but as that works both ways it may not be a problem. Star rating: *****

## Virgo meets Gemini

The fact that both these signs are ruled by the planet Mercury might at first seem good but, unfortunately, Mercury works very differently in these signs. Gemini is untidy, flighty, quick, changeable and easily bored, while Virgo is fastidious, steady and constant. If Virgo is willing to accept some anarchy all can be well, but this not usually the case. Virgoans are deep thinkers and may find Gemini a little superficial. This pair can be compatible intellectually, though even this side isn't without its problems. Star rating: ***

## Virgo meets Cancer

This match has little chance of success, for fairly simple reasons: Cancer's generous affection will be submerged by the Virgoan depths, not because Virgo is uncaring but because it expresses itself so differently. As both signs are naturally quiet, things might become a bit boring. They would be mutually supportive, possibly financially successful and have a very tidy house, but they won't share much sparkle, enthusiasm, risk-taking or passion. If this pair were stranded on a desert island, they might live at different ends of it. Star rating: **

## Virgo meets Leo

There is a chance for this couple, but it won't be trouble-free. Leo and Virgo view life very differently: Virgo is of a serious nature and struggles to relate to Leo's relentless optimism and cheerfulness and can find it annoying. Leo, meanwhile, may find Virgo stodgy, sometimes dark and uninspiring. The saving grace comes through communication – Leo knows how to make Virgo talk, which is what it needs. If this pair find happiness, though, it may be a case of opposites attract! Star rating: ***

# VENUS: THE PLANET OF LOVE

If you look up at the sky around sunset or sunrise you will often see Venus in close attendance to the Sun. It is arguably one of the most beautiful sights of all and there is little wonder that historically it became associated with the goddess of love. But although Venus does play an important part in the way you view love and in the way others see you romantically, this is only one of the spheres of influence that it enjoys in your overall character.

Venus has a part to play in the more cultured side of your life and has much to do with your appreciation of art, literature, music and general creativity. Even the way you look is responsive to the part of the zodiac that Venus occupied at the start of your life, though this fact is also down to your Sun sign and Ascending sign. If, at the time you were born, Venus occupied one of the more gregarious zodiac signs, you will be more likely to wear your heart on your sleeve, as well as to be more attracted to entertainment, social gatherings and good company. If on the other hand Venus occupied a quiet zodiac sign at the time of your birth, you would tend to be more retiring and less willing to shine in public situations.

It's good to know what part the planet Venus plays in your life, for it can have a great bearing on the way you appear to the rest of the world and since we all have to mix with others, you can learn to make the very best of what Venus has to offer you.

One of the great complications in the past has always been trying to establish exactly what zodiac position Venus enjoyed when you were born, because the planet is notoriously difficult to track. However, I have solved that problem by creating a table that is exclusive to your Sun sign, which you will find on the following page.

Establishing your Venus sign could not be easier. Just look up the year of your birth on the page opposite and you will see a sign of the Zodiac. This was the sign that Venus occupied in the period covered by your sign in that year. If Venus occupied more than one sign during the period, this is indicated by the date on which the sign changed, and the name of the new sign. For instance, if you were born in 1950, Venus was in Leo until the 10th September, after which time it was in Virgo. If you were born before 10th September your Venus sign is Leo, if you were born on or after 10th September, your Venus sign is Virgo. Once you have established the position of Venus at the time of your birth, you can then look in the pages which follow to see how this has a bearing on your life as a whole.

1917 LIBRA / 17.9 SCORPIO
1918 LEO / 12.9 VIRGO
1919 VIRGO
1920 VIRGO / 5.9 LIBRA
1921 CANCER / 31.8 LEO
1922 LIBRA / 8.9 SCORPIO
1923 LEO / 28.8 VIRGO / 20.9 LIBRA
1924 CANCER / 9.9 LEO
1925 LIBRA / 16.9 SCORPIO
1926 LEO / 12.9 VIRGO
1927 VIRGO
1928 VIRGO / 5.9 LIBRA
1929 CANCER / 31.8 LEO
1930 LIBRA / 7.9 SCORPIO
1931 LEO / 28.8 VIRGO / 20.9 LIBRA
1932 CANCER / 9.9 LEO
1933 LIBRA / 16.9 SCORPIO
1934 LEO / 11.9 VIRGO
1935 VIRGO
1936 VIRGO / 4.9 LIBRA
1937 CANCER / 31.8 LEO
1938 LIBRA / 7.9 SCORPIO
1939 LEO / 27.8 VIRGO / 19.9 LIBRA
1940 CANCER / 9.9 LEO
1941 LIBRA / 15.9 SCORPIO
1942 LEO / 11.9 VIRGO
1943 VIRGO
1944 VIRGO / 4.9 LIBRA
1945 CANCER / 30.8 LEO
1946 LIBRA / 7.9 SCORPIO
1947 LEO / 27.8 VIRGO / 18.9 LIBRA
1948 CANCER / 9.9 LEO
1949 LIBRA / 15.9 SCORPIO
1950 LEO / 10.9 VIRGO
1951 VIRGO
1952 VIRGO / 3.9 LIBRA
1953 CANCER / 30.8 LEO
1954 LIBRA / 7.9 SCORPIO
1955 LEO / 26.8 VIRGO / 17.9 LIBRA
1956 CANCER / 8.9 LEO
1957 LIBRA / 15.9 SCORPIO
1958 LEO / 10.9 VIRGO
1959 VIRGO / 20.9 LEO
1960 VIRGO / 3.9 LIBRA
1961 CANCER / 30.8 LEO
1962 LIBRA / 8.9 SCORPIO
1963 LEO / 26.8 VIRGO / 17.9 LIBRA
1964 CANCER / 8.9 LEO
1965 LIBRA / 15.9 SCORPIO
1966 LEO / 9.9 VIRGO
1967 VIRGO / 10.9 LEO
1968 VIRGO / 2.9 LIBRA
1969 CANCER / 29.8 LEO
1970 LIBRA / 8.9 SCORPIO
1971 LEO / 25.8 VIRGO / 16.9 LIBRA
1972 CANCER / 8.9 LEO
1973 LIBRA / 14.9 SCORPIO
1974 LEO / 8.9 VIRGO
1975 VIRGO / 3.9 LEO
1976 VIRGO / 2.9 LIBRA
1977 CANCER / 29.8 LEO
1978 LIBRA / 8.9 SCORPIO
1979 VIRGO / 16.9 LIBRA
1980 CANCER / 8.9 LEO
1981 LIBRA / 14.9 SCORPIO
1982 LEO / 7.9 VIRGO
1983 VIRGO / 28.8 LEO
1984 VIRGO / 2.9 LIBRA
1985 CANCER / 28.8 LEO
1986 LIBRA / 8.9 SCORPIO
1987 VIRGO / 15.9 LIBRA
1988 CANCER / 7.9 LEO
1989 LIBRA / 13.9 SCORPIO
1990 LEO / 7.9 VIRGO
1991 LEO
1992 VIRGO / 1.9 LIBRA
1993 CANCER / 28.8 LEO
1994 LIBRA / 8.9 SCORPIO
1995 VIRGO / 15.9 LIBRA
1996 CANCER / 7.9 LEO
1997 LIBRA / 12.9 SCORPIO
1998 LEO / 6.9 VIRGO
1999 LEO
2000 VIRGO / 1.9 LIBRA
2001 CANCER / 28.8 LEO
2002 LIBRA / 8.9 SCORPIO
2003 VIRGO / 15.9 LIBRA
2004 CANCER / 6.9 LEO
2005 LIBRA / 10.9 SCORPIO
2006 LEO / 4.9 VIRGO
2007 LEO
2008 VIRGO / 1.9 LIBRA
2009 CANCER / 28.8 LEO
2010 LIBRA / 8.9 SCORPIO
2011 VIRGO / 15.9 LIBRA
2012 CANCER / 6.9 LEO
2013 LIBRA / 10.9 SCORPIO
2014 LEO / 4.9 VIRGO
2015 LEO

# VENUS THROUGH THE ZODIAC SIGNS

## Venus in Aries

Amongst other things, the position of Venus in Aries indicates a fondness for travel, music and all creative pursuits. Your nature tends to be affectionate and you would try not to create confusion or difficulty for others if it could be avoided. Many people with this planetary position have a great love of the theatre, and mental stimulation is of the greatest importance. Early romantic attachments are common with Venus in Aries, so it is very important to establish a genuine sense of romantic continuity. Early marriage is not recommended, especially if it is based on sympathy. You may give your heart a little too readily on occasions.

## Venus in Taurus

You are capable of very deep feelings and your emotions tend to last for a very long time. This makes you a trusting partner and lover, whose constancy is second to none. In life you are precise and careful and always try to do things the right way. Although this means an ordered life, which you are comfortable with, it can also lead you to be rather too fussy for your own good. Despite your pleasant nature, you are very fixed in your opinions and quite able to speak your mind. Others are attracted to you and historical astrologers always quoted this position of Venus as being very fortunate in terms of marriage. However, if you find yourself involved in a failed relationship, it could take you a long time to trust again.

## Venus in Gemini

As with all associations related to Gemini, you tend to be quite versatile, anxious for change and intelligent in your dealings with the world at large. You may gain money from more than one source but you are equally good at spending it. There is an inference here that you are a good communicator, via either the written or the spoken word, and you love to be in the company of interesting people. Always on the look-out for culture, you may also be very fond of music, and love to indulge the curious and cultured side of your nature. In romance you tend to have more than one relationship and could find yourself associated with someone who has previously been a friend or even a distant relative.

## Venus in Cancer

You often stay close to home because you are very fond of family and enjoy many of your most treasured moments when you are with those you love. Being naturally sympathetic, you will always do anything you can to support those around you, even people you hardly know at all. This charitable side of your nature is your most noticeable trait and is one of the reasons why others are naturally so fond of you. Being receptive and in some cases even psychic, you can see through to the soul of most of those with whom you come into contact. You may not commence too many romantic attachments but when you do give your heart, it tends to be unconditionally.

## Venus in Leo

It must become quickly obvious to almost anyone you meet that you are kind, sympathetic and yet determined enough to stand up for anyone or anything that is truly important to you. Bright and sunny, you warm the world with your natural enthusiasm and would rarely do anything to hurt those around you, or at least not intentionally. In romance you are ardent and sincere, though some may find your style just a little overpowering. Gains come through your contacts with other people and this could be especially true with regard to romance, for love and money often come hand in hand for those who were born with Venus in Leo. People claim to understand you, though you are more complex than you seem.

## Venus in Virgo

Your nature could well be fairly quiet no matter what your Sun sign might be, though this fact often manifests itself as an inner peace and would not prevent you from being basically sociable. Some delays and even the odd disappointment in love cannot be ruled out with this planetary position, though it's a fact that you will usually find the happiness you look for in the end. Catapulting yourself into romantic entanglements that you know to be rather ill-advised is not sensible, and it would be better to wait before you committed yourself exclusively to any one person. It is the essence of your nature to serve the world at large and through doing so it is possible that you will attract money at some stage in your life.

## Venus in Libra

Venus is very comfortable in Libra and bestows upon those people who have this planetary position a particular sort of kindness that is easy to recognise. This is a very good position for all sorts of friendships and also for romantic attachments that usually bring much joy into your life. Few individuals with Venus in Libra would avoid marriage and since you are capable of great depths of love, it is likely that you will find a contented personal life. You like to mix with people of integrity and intelligence but don't take kindly to scruffy surroundings or work that means getting your hands too dirty. Careful speculation, good business dealings and money through marriage all seem fairly likely.

## Venus in Scorpio

You are quite open and tend to spend money quite freely, even on those occasions when you don't have very much. Although your intentions are always good, there are times when you get yourself in to the odd scrape and this can be particularly true when it comes to romance, which you may come to late or from a rather unexpected direction. Certainly you have the power to be happy and to make others contented on the way, but you find the odd stumbling block on your journey through life and it could seem that you have to work harder than those around you. As a result of this, you gain a much deeper understanding of the true value of personal happiness than many people ever do, and are likely to achieve true contentment in the end.

## Venus in Sagittarius

You are lighthearted, cheerful and always able to see the funny side of any situation. These facts enhance your popularity, which is especially high with members of the opposite sex. You should never have to look too far to find romantic interest in your life, though it is just possible that you might be too willing to commit yourself before you are certain that the person in question is right for you. Part of the problem here extends to other areas of life too. The fact is that you like variety in everything and so can tire of situations that fail to offer it. All the same, if you choose wisely and learn to understand your restless side, then great happiness can be yours.

## Venus in Capricorn

The most notable trait that comes from Venus in this position is that it makes you trustworthy and able to take on all sorts of responsibilities in life. People are instinctively fond of you and love you all the more because you are always ready to help those who are in any form of need. Social and business popularity can be yours and there is a magnetic quality to your nature that is particularly attractive in a romantic sense. Anyone who wants a partner for a lover, a spouse and a good friend too would almost certainly look in your direction. Constancy is the hallmark of your nature and unfaithfulness would go right against the grain. You might sometimes be a little too trusting.

## Venus in Aquarius

This location of Venus offers a fondness for travel and a desire to try out something new at every possible opportunity. You are extremely easy to get along with and tend to have many friends from varied backgrounds, classes and inclinations. You like to live a distinct sort of life and gain a great deal from moving about, both in a career sense and with regard to your home. It is not out of the question that you could form a romantic attachment to someone who comes from far away or be attracted to a person of a distinctly artistic and original nature. What you cannot stand is jealousy, for you have friends of both sexes and would want to keep things that way.

## Venus in Pisces

The first thing people tend to notice about you is your wonderful, warm smile. Being very charitable by nature you will do anything to help others, even if you don't know them well. Much of your life may be spent sorting out situations for other people, but it is very important to feel that you are living for yourself too. In the main, you remain cheerful, and tend to be quite attractive to members of the opposite sex. Where romantic attachments are concerned, you could be drawn to people who are significantly older or younger than yourself or to someone with a unique career or point of view. It might be best for you to avoid marrying whilst you are still very young.

# HOW THE DIAGRAMS WORK

Through the picture diagrams in the Astral Diary I want to help you to plot your year. With them you can see where the positive and negative aspects will be found in each month. To make the most of them, all you have to do is remember where and when!

Let me show you how they work ...

## THE MONTH AT A GLANCE

Just as there are twelve separate zodiac signs, so astrologers believe that each sign has twelve separate aspects to life. Each of the twelve segments relates to a different personal aspect. I list them all every month so that their meanings are always clear.

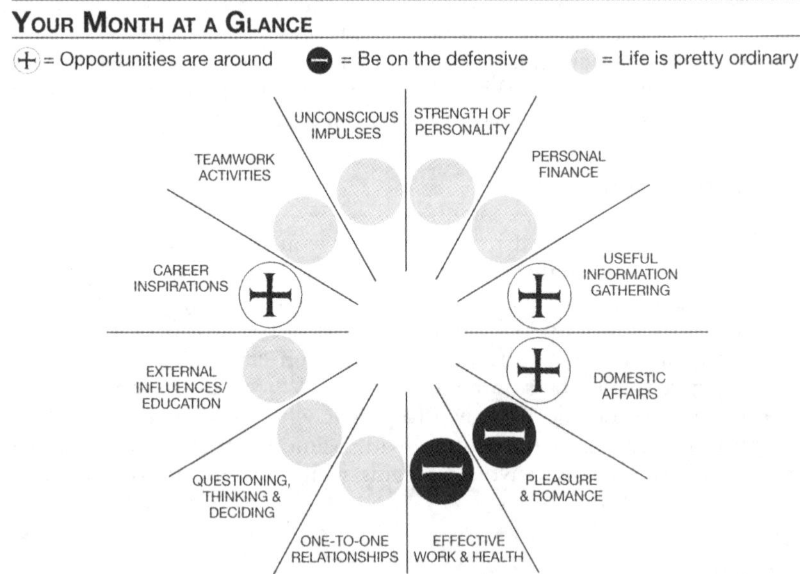


I have designed this chart to show you how and when these twelve different aspects are being influenced throughout the year. When there is a shaded circle, nothing out of the ordinary is to be expected. However, when a circle turns white with a plus sign, the influence is positive. Where the circle is black with a minus sign, it is a negative.

## YOUR ENERGY RHYTHM CHART

Below is a picture diagram in which I link your zodiac group to the rhythm of the Moon. In doing this I have calculated when you will be gaining strength from its influence and equally when you may be weakened by it.

If you think of yourself as being like the tides of the ocean then you may understand how your own energies must also rise and fall. And if you understand how it works and when it is working, then you can better organise your activities to achieve more and get things done more easily.

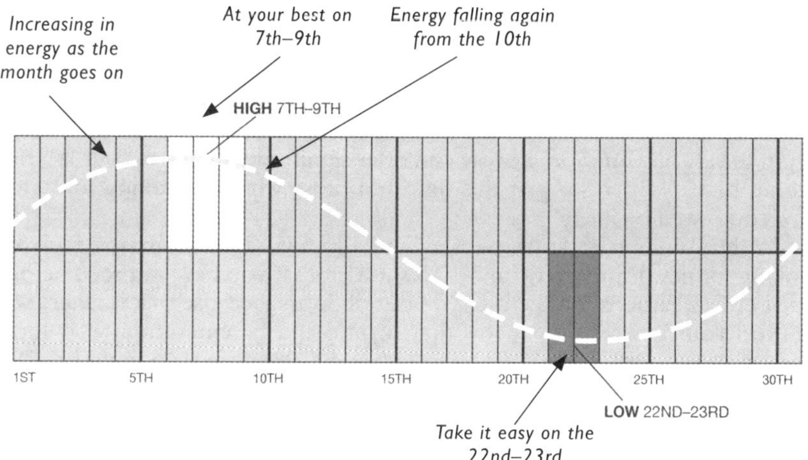


## THE KEY DAYS

Some of the entries are in **bold**, which indicates the working of astrological cycles in your life. Look out for them each week as they are the best days to take action or make decisions. The daily text tells you which area of your life to focus on.

## MERCURY RETROGRADE

The Mercury symbol (☿) indicates that Mercury is retrograde on that day. Since Mercury governs communication, the fact that it appears to be moving backwards when viewed from the Earth at this time should warn you that your communication skills are not likely to be at their best and you could expect some setbacks.

# VIRGO: YOUR YEAR IN BRIEF

Don't be too quick to jump to conclusions at the beginning of the year, but instead try your best to wait for matters to sort themselves out before you interfere. January and February see you working hard in order to attain your most longed-for objectives, but the winter weather won't please you and some Virgo people will be anxious to fly off to the sun. Finance is well starred towards the end of February.

March and April should prove to be slightly more eventful and might bring you to a better understanding of issues that have been on your mind for some time. You think clearly and act positively, so much so that others begin to rely on you more heavily and offer significant support. Your love life should be very interesting at this time and those who are looking for a new love could well be lucky.

As the summer beckons, so May and June will be inclined to find you looking for new things to do and places to visit that you have not seen before. The better weather should entice you out of doors, because that is where you will feel your greatest joy at this time. You could be entering a fairly lucky streak and can probably afford to speculate a little more than would usually be the case. There are many personalities entering your life at this time.

July and August should prove to be quite eventful as opportunities open up for you. Friends are especially important at this time, and you will be extremely social and sociable. This means being put in the spotlight on occasions, and although being out there in the public gaze isn't always your thing, you will deal well enough with the situation at this time. This is a good period for writing and speaking.

It is during September and October that you may come to realise just how capable you can be. During both of these months you are likely to discover skills you didn't know you possessed and your abilities will certainly impress other people. Personal attachments mean more to you at this stage of the year and some Virgo people could be finding new love under October's autumn star. Don't be too shy to tell people how important they are to you.

November and December, might at first sight seem the least helpful to you, because a number of obstacles are being put in your path. However, it is by resolving these that you come to a much better understanding of yourself and of life. The Christmas period should be packed with possibilities and may not turn out at all the way you expected. Finish the year with a flourish and in possession of your usual optimism about the future, as well as on a lunar high.

## Your Month at a Glance

(+) = Opportunities are around (−) = Be on the defensive ( ) = Life is pretty ordinary

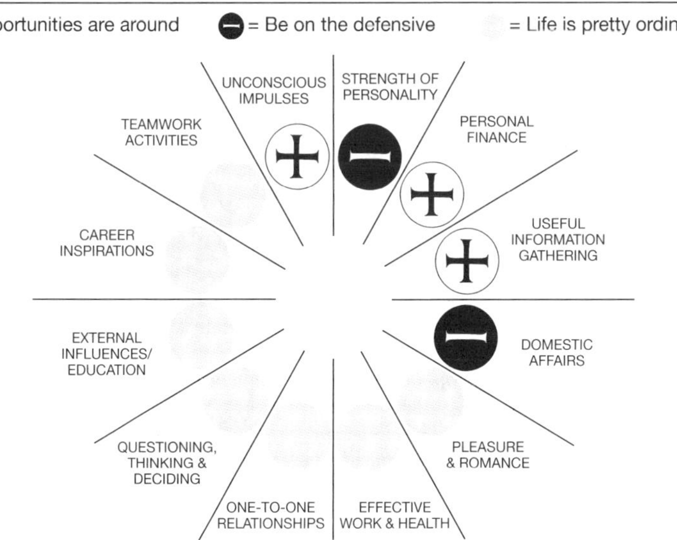


## January Highs and Lows

*Here I show you how the rhythms of the Moon will affect you this month. Like the tide, your energies and abilities will rise and fall with its pattern. When it is above the centre line, go for it, when it is below, you should be resting.*

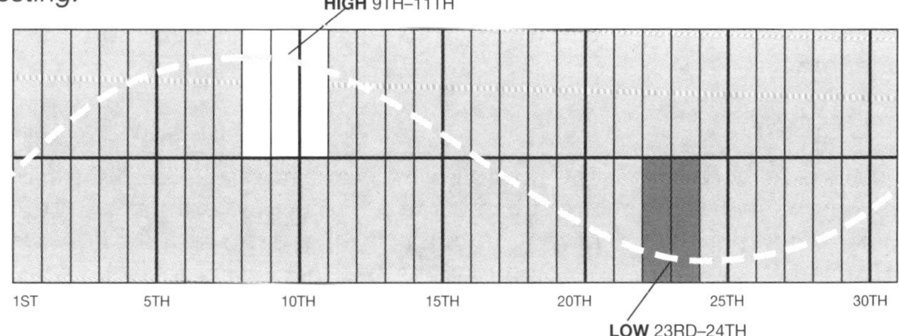

## 1 THURSDAY *Moon Age Day 11 Moon Sign Taurus*

A personal matter needs extra patience and the sort of overview that you are able to offer. Much of your thinking is now geared towards house and home, with the result that the more practical aspects could be taking a back seat. You may decide that the time is right to brush up your life, perhaps in terms of personal fitness.

## 2 FRIDAY *Moon Age Day 12 Moon Sign Gemini*

A professional matter now proves to be very uplifting, as you discover the right way to go about a particular task that might have been something of a mystery to you until now. Concentration becomes easier, as you settle down and accept that this is a new year and that life could prove to be somewhat different now.

## 3 SATURDAY *Moon Age Day 13 Moon Sign Gemini*

This is an excellent weekend for putting your point of view across to others. Once you have stated your case, allow matters to rest and don't push issues too much. Enjoy yourself doing those things that suit you, but don't get too carried away with routines and traditions. Times are changing and you have to change with them.

## 4 SUNDAY *Moon Age Day 14 Moon Sign Gemini*

Do your best to avoid minor accidents in the home. There are signs that you should be aware of what you are doing and, if possible, avoid any form of DIY just for the moment. As far as your personal life is concerned, it might appear that you cannot put a foot wrong. Don't worry, someone will find a way to contradict that opinion!

## 5 MONDAY *Moon Age Day 15 Moon Sign Cancer*

Large gatherings appeal to you at the moment. Socially or professionally, it seems that you are in full flow and your powers of communication are emphasised as a result. This isn't perhaps the time you would choose to take a day off, but you might tend to burn the candle at both ends more than is good for you.

## 6 TUESDAY *Moon Age Day 16 Moon Sign Cancer*

You need to be aware of the possibility of being driven by emotion-based habits now, something that can happen to Virgo people from time to time. Look for new possibilities in your life and be willing to go with the flow, even if that sometimes appears to be the wrong direction. This could be a good time for change.

## 7 WEDNESDAY
*Moon Age Day 17 Moon Sign Leo*

The more the merrier is the adage today, both in terms of the jobs you are taking on and with regard to the number of people you are entertaining in your life. It doesn't matter whether you know folk that well or not at present. Communication skills are good and you are able to come to terms with a few past errors.

## 8 THURSDAY
*Moon Age Day 18 Moon Sign Leo*

It could be said that getting what you want from life today is more important than almost anything else. Unfortunately, this makes you sound quite selfish, which isn't the case at all. On the contrary, most of what you want involves a better life for others, even if you do feather your own nest on the way.

## 9 FRIDAY
*Moon Age Day 19 Moon Sign Virgo*

**The Moon is back in your zodiac sign. That means a get-up-and-go sort of period, one that is typified by high energy levels and an irrepressible desire to be out there in the thick of things. In terms of experiences, quality is as important as quality, though you could manage to get a little of both today.**

## 10 SATURDAY
*Moon Age Day 20 Moon Sign Virgo*

**Future plans can give you a shot in the arm as the weekend begins. In fact, most Virgo subjects could start Saturday with a flourish. Even though not all news appears to be good, you can still make the best of it. Rummage around to find clothes that you can put back into service, because you arc ingenious now.**

## 11 SUNDAY
*Moon Age Day 21 Moon Sign Virgo*

**Get out and about as much as you can today. It does you good to mix and mingle with others, despite the winter weather. In any case, a change is as good as a rest, particularly if that means you are coming together with the sort of people who find you very attractive. Concentrate on money matters later in the day.**

## 12 MONDAY
*Moon Age Day 22 Moon Sign Libra*

This is a forward-looking period and one that finds you focused on mainstream life, rushing on towards specific objectives. It is clear that you know what you want from life and how to go about getting it. Try to make your home more comfortable and listen to family members who have an important tale to tell.

## 13 TUESDAY *Moon Age Day 23 Moon Sign Libra*

This might be seen by others as a fairly self-indulgent time for Virgo. It's a facet of your nature that does crop up time and again, which is why Virgoans often have to watch what they eat. There is no real tendency towards selfishness, but you can sometimes be short of confidence. Don't turn to the Mars bars.

## 14 WEDNESDAY *Moon Age Day 24 Moon Sign Scorpio*

However long a particular task takes is the time you have to spend on it. That is self-evident to you, but probably not so in the case of other people. There is a deep and profound spirituality about your thinking at the moment, which could lead others to seek you out for help and advice.

## 15 THURSDAY *Moon Age Day 25 Moon Sign Scorpio*

You find it easy to bend career situations the way you would wish and so it might be best not to try, at least for the moment. Concentrating on the matter at hand won't be too easy and you need to be aware of the broader picture of life, in any case. Something or someone very unusual might come into your world soon.

## 16 FRIDAY *Moon Age Day 26 Moon Sign Scorpio*

Romance and personal relationships represent the area of life that might appeal the most right now. In a practical sense, there isn't too much you can do to make a splash, though looking ahead and planning isn't going to be a waste of time. What would really suit you down to the ground would be a change of scene.

## 17 SATURDAY *Moon Age Day 27 Moon Sign Sagittarius*

Although it might sometimes appear that the progress you make is limited, nothing could be further from the truth. You have a very positive attitude, especially if you are at work, and might be singled out for some significant attention from superiors. Extra responsibilities are not out of the question.

## 18 SUNDAY *Moon Age Day 28 Moon Sign Sagittarius*

There are times to argue, and periods when it is better to keep your own counsel. The latter is the case right now, so don't get involved unless you are forced. However, if you have no choice but to express your opinions, you should do so with all the clarity and conviction presently in your arsenal.

## 19 MONDAY *Moon Age Day 29 Moon Sign Capricorn*

Look out for a distinct advantage at work today, and don't be afraid to exploit it for all you are worth. There are people around who are in an excellent position to lend you a hand and you should not be too proud to make use of their services. When it comes to spending money, you need to be just a little careful.

## 20 TUESDAY *Moon Age Day 0 Moon Sign Capricorn*

Keep away from the sort of people who have a history of failure and disaster behind them, particularly if they are asking you for money. All in all, this is a time to keep your purse or wallet tightly closed. If you have to sign any documents at the moment, it would be good to read the small print very carefully indeed.

## 21 WEDNESDAY *Moon Age Day 1 Moon Sign Aquarius*

There are some exciting and interesting possibilities in store for you at present. Look around you and see where the river of life wants to take you, because you can get much of what you want without having to try all that hard. Convictions are important today, but don't take them to extremes.

## 22 THURSDAY ☿ *Moon Age Day 2 Moon Sign Aquarius*

Make use of the strong supporting elements around you at the moment. It is likely that one or two people think a great deal of you, and are willing to say so in public. Be willing to stand up for someone who is in trouble, even if you have to put yourself out significantly to do so.

## 23 FRIDAY ☿ *Moon Age Day 3 Moon Sign Pisces*

It seems to be time to slow down and to take a break. You might be feeling somewhat lacking in lustre and can blame the position of the Moon for this state of affairs. Lunar lows are not usually too much of a problem to Virgo, which has a strong tendency to retreat into itself on occasion in any case.

## 24 SATURDAY ☿ *Moon Age Day 4 Moon Sign Pisces*

The position of the Moon could put a slight damper on particular wishes you have for today. There is no point at all in trying to move mountains. Things will come right when the time is at hand and it doesn't matter what you do, that is the case now. Simply enjoy sitting and watching the river of life today.

## 25 SUNDAY ☿ *Moon Age Day 5 Moon Sign Aries*

A rather idealistic frame of mind might colour your judgements on this Sunday. It is true that the lunar low has passed, making you feel rather more energetic. However, you need to realise what is realistic in the short term and what can easily wait until a later date. Creative potential looks especially good at this time.

## 26 MONDAY ☿ *Moon Age Day 6 Moon Sign Aries*

Good progress is possible, though it can be somewhat restricted by a slightly negative attitude on your part if you are mixing with people who seem reluctant to give their all to situations. Be careful who you ally yourself with right now and, if possible, stick with those who have success tattooed all over them.

## 27 TUESDAY ☿ *Moon Age Day 7 Moon Sign Taurus*

If there is one thing that is bound to get on your nerves at present, it is others telling you how you ought to live your life. Unfortunately, you don't have much option but to listen. Trends opposing solo pursuits mean you genuinely do need the support that those around you can offer.

## 28 WEDNESDAY ☿ *Moon Age Day 8 Moon Sign Taurus*

Confidence is lacking in projects you don't understand, which is why it would be sensible for the moment to stick to some good old favourites. Creative potential is good, especially around the home, but you also need to have hobbies and pastimes of your own, which is something to think about now.

## 29 THURSDAY ☿ *Moon Age Day 9 Moon Sign Gemini*

A broad view of your life now leads to certain changes that you want to make. Don't be afraid to be off with the old and on with the new, even if you find that this means a good deal of upheaval. The year of 2015 brings changes into your life, so you might as well be in charge of them.

## 30 FRIDAY ☿ *Moon Age Day 10 Moon Sign Gemini*

The trouble with today is that there is a host of things to do and maybe not enough time to fit everything in. This is where planning is important. Right now, it is definitely better to do one task well, rather than to botch half a dozen. If the weather is fair, a good walk would almost certainly do you good.

## 31 SATURDAY ☿ *Moon Age Day 11 Moon Sign Gemini*

Due to higher levels of physical energy today, it is clear that you are more willing to be out there at the front. Any form of sporting activity is well highlighted, and you wouldn't even mind being put on the spot in social situations at this time. Creative potential tends to be very good.

# February

2015

## Your Month at a Glance

+ = Opportunities are around   – = Be on the defensive   = Life is pretty ordinary

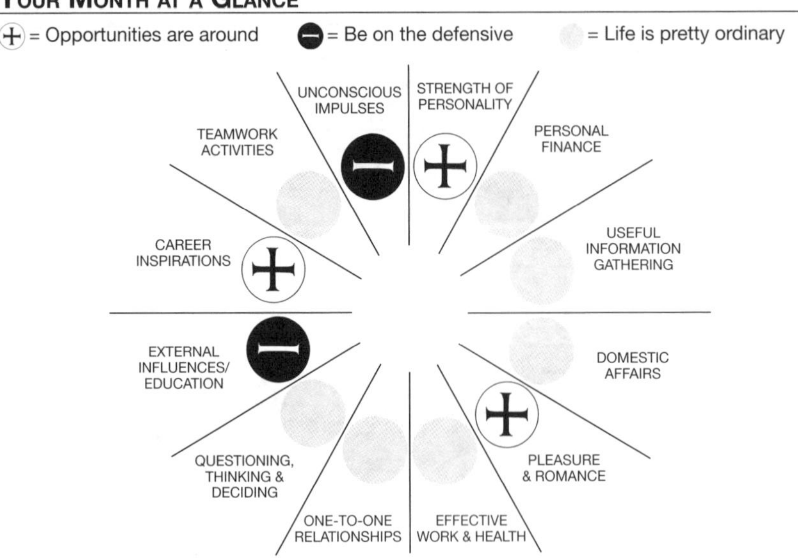


## February Highs and Lows

*Here I show you how the rhythms of the Moon will affect you this month. Like the tide, your energies and abilities will rise and fall with its pattern. When it is above the centre line, go for it, when it is below, you should be resting.*

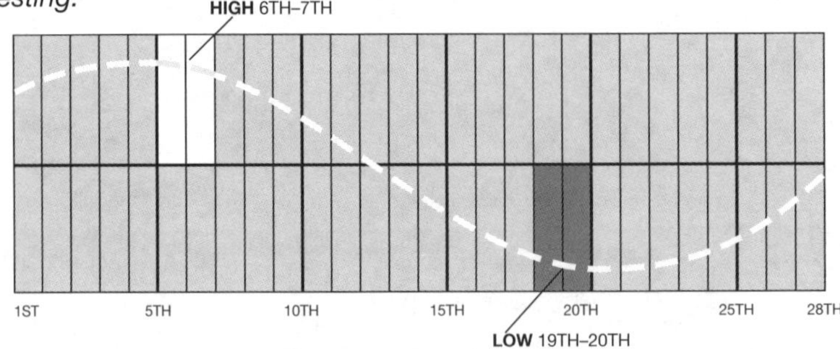

## 1 SUNDAY ☿ *Moon Age Day 12 Moon Sign Cancer*

Though you are more than ready to form new contacts of one sort or another today, you should avoid coming on too strong. Confidence is important, but you might give certain people the wrong impression. A healthy dose of humility does more for you now than a brash approach.

## 2 MONDAY ☿ *Moon Age Day 13 Moon Sign Cancer*

It's true that you have to work quite hard now the get the good things of life, but being a Virgo that doesn't worry you too much. Look out for the help and support of friends, some of whom have a good idea or two that, in the fullness of time, could make you significantly better off than you are now.

## 3 TUESDAY ☿ *Moon Age Day 14 Moon Sign Leo*

Getting ahead today depends on a degree of specialised knowledge, which in one form or another we all have. Ask yourself what you know about that others do not and concentrate on those matters. Somewhere within them lies the opportunity for you to get on better and perhaps even make some money. Be supportive of friends who are in trouble.

## 4 WEDNESDAY ☿ *Moon Age Day 15 Moon Sign Leo*

Be aware of planetary trends simulating the competitive side of your nature. There's nothing especially wrong with that, just as long as you are thinking things through clearly and soundly. Don't give in to impulses to overdo things, particularly when the jobs concerned are entirely voluntary.

## 5 THURSDAY ☿ *Moon Age Day 16 Moon Sign Leo*

Although many of the opportunities that come your way today prove to be small in scope, the end result is likely to prove very positive. It is all a matter of looking carefully and then concentrating on one task at once. No matter how unlikely it looks, you can engender a greater influence over your own life now.

## 6 FRIDAY ☿ *Moon Age Day 17 Moon Sign Virgo*

**This can be a very good day for making progress. There are new inroads planned into special projects that are very close to your heart. Something you have been thinking about for a while can now become a reality and it clearly has financial implications. You don't look for security today, and are in the market for excitement.**

## 7 SATURDAY ☿ *Moon Age Day 18 Moon Sign Virgo*

**Even if you are being very successful at present, this is no time for being complacent. It is true that you have a superior sort of judgement, but you need to use it in a very progressive manner. The outcome of recent efforts allows you to make more of yourself and to show an extremely positive face to the world.**

## 8 SUNDAY ☿ *Moon Age Day 19 Moon Sign Libra*

There are improvements to be made in your career, though it could be difficult to monitor the situation specifically on a Sunday. This would be a good day for shopping or for spending some time in the company of lively and articulate friends. What you don't need at the moment is grumpy types.

## 9 MONDAY ☿ *Moon Age Day 20 Moon Sign Libra*

A time of high spirits is clearly at hand. Things that are going on in the outside world should lift your spirits nicely. Freedom is the key to happiness and you will find yourself able to get through or over obstacles that have blocked your path for quite some time. What helps is that you are now being so realistic.

## 10 TUESDAY ☿ *Moon Age Day 21 Moon Sign Libra*

Social matters ought to prove highly stimulating and you can enjoy the company of a number of different sorts of people. You need to balance outside activities with pressing work obligations, in which you might be slipping behind a little. There should be plenty of time for enjoyment in the evening.

## 11 WEDNESDAY ☿ *Moon Age Day 22 Moon Sign Scorpio*

This is a very fruitful period for friendships and for finding people with whom you instinctively feel you have much in common. Some patience will be necessary regarding a specific enterprise, but people probably won't keep you waiting that long. A degree of ingenuity is what is called for at this time.

## 12 THURSDAY ☿ *Moon Age Day 23 Moon Sign Scorpio*

Inside, you might be quaking at the thought of some contact or approach you now have to make, but this is absolutely necessary if you want to make more of yourself in the days and weeks ahead. Summon up all your courage and move forward. The people you fear are by no means ogres.

## 13 FRIDAY ☿ *Moon Age Day 24 Moon Sign Sagittarius*

Activities in the outer world should prove to be quite fulfilling. At the same time, there is enjoyment to be found at home, so you could be quite torn as to what to do with your day. Decision-making isn't difficult. Your nature at the moment is calm and steady, which is typical of the best attributes of your zodiac sign.

## 14 SATURDAY *Moon Age Day 25 Moon Sign Sagittarius*

Love life and romantic matters are continuing to show a distinct improvement. In a more practical sense, this is no time to be hiding your light under a bushel. If you know what you are talking about in any given situation, now is the time to speak out, even though it can take some courage to do so.

## 15 SUNDAY *Moon Age Day 26 Moon Sign Capricorn*

Self-confidence isn't lacking, but the means to get everything you want from life may not be present today. You need to be innovative and to think on your feet. People you haven't seen for ages are likely to come back into your life at this time and might bring some important news with them.

## 16 MONDAY *Moon Age Day 27 Moon Sign Capricorn*

When it comes to professional matters, you can be quite successful this week. With tremendous perception and an instinct with regard to what is likely to work for you, it's time to put your best foot forward. On the romantic front, you may find that new offers are on the way – that is, if you are interested in them.

## 17 TUESDAY *Moon Age Day 28 Moon Sign Aquarius*

There can be a few ups and downs in finances now. All the more reason to spend wisely and after due thought. This is a good time for romantic encounters, and especially so for Virgo people who are not tied down to a specific relationship. Others find you intriguing now.

## 18 WEDNESDAY *Moon Age Day 29 Moon Sign Aquarius*

Your personality profile is running high and this is definitely the right time to go for what you want. Few people would refuse you at present, and where awkward types do appear, your natural personality can bring them round in a flash. Conforming to expectations is boring to you now and you love to surprise people.

## 19 THURSDAY *Moon Age Day 0 Moon Sign Pisces*

You cannot get away entirely from the presence of the lunar low today. For a sign such as Virgo, the presence of the Moon in your opposite zodiac sign is not always particularly apparent. However, you may notice that life is not proceeding quite as smoothly as has recently been the case and extra effort is required.

## 20 FRIDAY *Moon Age Day 1 Moon Sign Pisces*

Once again, you will register the fact that things are not working out entirely as you might wish. An extra dose of self-created enthusiasm gets you through any minor difficulties now and there are new incentives coming your way before the day is out. The most promising aspects of your life are social in nature.

## 21 SATURDAY *Moon Age Day 2 Moon Sign Aries*

Someone is bugging you right now, and there appears to be very little you can do about the situation. It would be better by far to ignore what you cannot alter and to get on with something different instead. There are gains to be made financially, though probably not through gambling or any form of speculation.

## 22 SUNDAY *Moon Age Day 3 Moon Sign Aries*

Retrieving what you can from difficult situations will enable you make the best of everything today. You won't be let down by the actions of your friends, one or two of whom prove to be extremely supportive. Create a friendly atmosphere whenever you can and be willing to put yourself out, even for a stranger.

## 23 MONDAY *Moon Age Day 4 Moon Sign Aries*

Rules and regulations are necessary, and you are not against inventing a few yourself on occasion. However, you don't always follow them and certainly don't at the moment. There is an impish quality to your nature that allows you to wring humour out of any situations, professional, personal or social.

## 24 TUESDAY *Moon Age Day 5 Moon Sign Taurus*

You still seem to be progressing well, but you need to be aware that not everyone is working to your advantage. Keep an open mind about friends who call for your support. Though you might think one or two of them have been foolish, you can still be prevailed upon to help them out.

## 25 WEDNESDAY *Moon Age Day 6 Moon Sign Taurus*

This may not be the most exciting Wednesday you will ever know, but it can be fairly solid all the same. Don't try anything too outrageous and if you have to work, follow the lead of people who are in the know. Keep your ideas to yourself for today, but be prepared to put them into practice soon.

## 26 THURSDAY *Moon Age Day 7 Moon Sign Gemini*

Virgo is on fine form at this stage of the week, particularly in a romantic sense. Be prepared to sweep someone off his or her feet and don't be averse to a little lighthearted flirting, no matter what your marital state. It does you good now and again to realise that you are more than attractive to some folk.

## 27 FRIDAY *Moon Age Day 8 Moon Sign Gemini*

There are advantages about if you know where to look for them. Contrary to popular belief, things are turning your way financially, whilst the social scene should look extremely interesting at this time. When it comes to impressing those around you, actions speak louder than words.

## 28 SATURDAY *Moon Age Day 9 Moon Sign Cancer*

Confidence remains intact for much of the weekend, though you might find one or two problems coming from the direction of family members. If this turns out to be the case, solve them as early in the day as you can. After that, you will feel the need for a change of scene and for social diversity.

# March

2015

## Your Month at a Glance

(+) = Opportunities are around (−) = Be on the defensive ( ) = Life is pretty ordinary

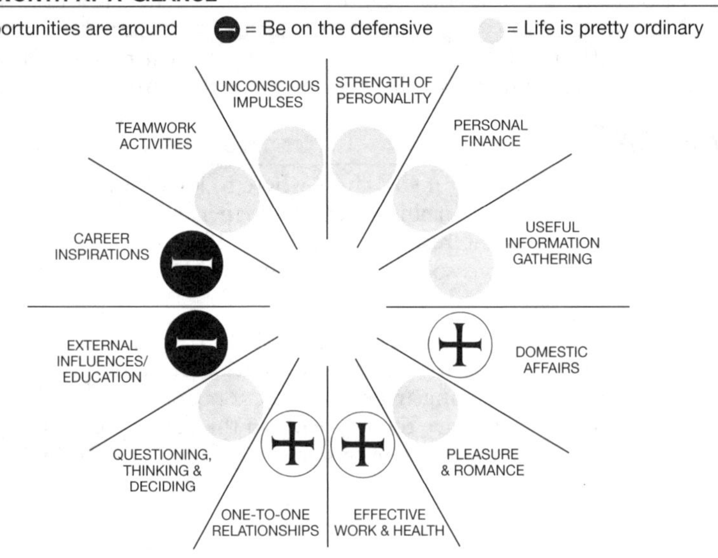


## March Highs and Lows

*Here I show you how the rhythms of the Moon will affect you this month. Like the tide, your energies and abilities will rise and fall with its pattern. When it is above the centre line, go for it, when it is below, you should be resting.*

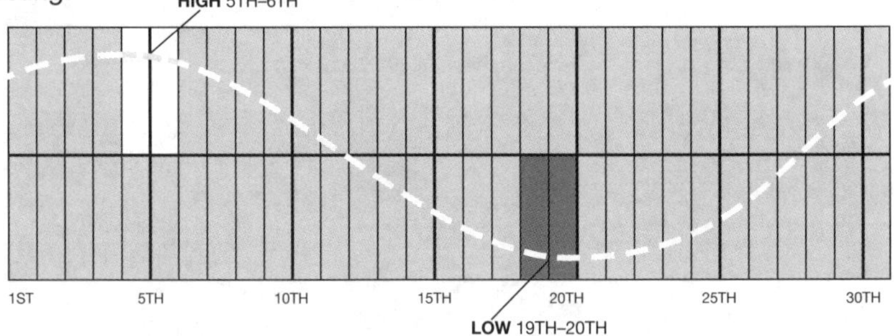

## 1 SUNDAY
*Moon Age Day 10 Moon Sign Cancer*

A wild and carefree Virgo subject is likely to meet the dawn of this day. You are filled with prospects for excitement and would be unlikely to allow any given obstacle to get in your way for very long. Arguments are not helpful now, especially in the family. Do just about anything to avoid them.

## 2 MONDAY
*Moon Age Day 11 Moon Sign Leo*

With an eye to the future and good powers of communication at your disposal, this is hardly likely to be the sort of Monday to stay at home and mope. It's true that you might have to make most of the running, but that fact probably won't bother you at all. Give yourself credit for recent successes and soldier on anyway.

## 3 TUESDAY
*Moon Age Day 12 Moon Sign Leo*

This is a beneficial phase that should bring your communication skills to the fore. With plenty going your way and life looking pretty good, you will be feeling fine and able to deal with just about any challenge that comes your way. Keep a sense of proportion over small financial losses.

## 4 WEDNESDAY
*Moon Age Day 13 Moon Sign Leo*

Confidence grows gradually, but certainly isn't at its height today. You may decide that the time is right to do some planning and to look ahead of yourself in practical issues. This is not really a day for taking risks, though this state of affairs is likely to change in only a few hours. Make the most of the evening.

## 5 THURSDAY
*Moon Age Day 14 Moon Sign Virgo*

**Acting on impulse is part of what the lunar high inspires you to do. Under most circumstances today you simply go for what you want and manage to obtain it. It looks as though you are likely to be more dominant, though not in a way that is likely to upset anyone else in your vicinity.**

## 6 FRIDAY
*Moon Age Day 15 Moon Sign Virgo*

**Up early and keen to meet life head on, the lunar high inspires you to be far more determined regarding plans that have been in your mind for some time. Confidence should not be lacking and even personal relationships prove to be an area in which you are able to bring people round to your point of view.**

## 7 SATURDAY *Moon Age Day 16 Moon Sign Libra*

The accent is now on the domestic scene and you turn your attention towards matters associated with house and home. The future looks bright ahead of you and for much of the time you will be very busy. As a result, you may choose to spend more time with family members, since you won't have much time later.

## 8 SUNDAY *Moon Age Day 17 Moon Sign Libra*

Prepare to make a rather positive impact on people who can be of great use to you later. Stay away from jobs that bore you and try to do those things that can be exciting and different. A complete change of scene would suit you down the ground, and could get you noticed by some attractive and interesting people.

## 9 MONDAY *Moon Age Day 18 Moon Sign Libra*

Some setbacks at work can be expected, but you have the ability to turn them around. Now and again today, you will find yourself up against people who seem determined to be awkward. The best way to deal with them is to show them your present charming character, which can be totally disarming.

## 10 TUESDAY *Moon Age Day 19 Moon Sign Scorpio*

You are in a very positive frame of mind today and stand a chance of making a good deal more progress as a result. What might be even more important is your ability to turn heads and to make other people notice you. This can help you in a work sense, but also personally, too.

## 11 WEDNESDAY *Moon Age Day 20 Moon Sign Scorpio*

This is one of the most pleasurable days of the month as far as social matters are concerned. It's a pity if you have to work, because now you really do want to have fun. Even if you are tied down by responsibility through the day, you will be redressing the balance before very long.

## 12 THURSDAY *Moon Age Day 21 Moon Sign Sagittarius*

It could be that social and romantic offers are going very much your way right now. You tend to be in the good books of most people, and particularly one or two who appear very attractive when viewed from your side of the fence. Curb a tendency to be too outspoken, especially about matters you don't understand.

## 13 FRIDAY *Moon Age Day 22 Moon Sign Sagittarius*

Now you find yourself running around frantically, trying to get things done that should have been completed before. In all probability, you only have yourself to blame and you know it. Nevertheless, you remain generally good-natured and friendly. Virgo is capable of great charm this Friday, and people will remember.

## 14 SATURDAY *Moon Age Day 23 Moon Sign Sagittarius*

Make sure others don't misconstrue what you are saying. Even if it means repeating yourself on a number of occasions this weekend, you can come through in the end. What a good day this would be to go out shopping, or to find something in the wardrobe you had forgotten you even owned.

## 15 SUNDAY *Moon Age Day 24 Moon Sign Capricorn*

You are happiest today when taking something of a back seat. Letting other people have their head now and again is no bad thing. Besides, you have an ulterior motive. If you make yourself look less than capable, especially at home, someone will come along and do some of the jobs you haven't been looking forward to.

## 16 MONDAY *Moon Age Day 25 Moon Sign Capricorn*

A demanding and high-energy period kicks off the start of this new working week. Filled with vitality and simply raring to get stuck in, there is nobody around who could possibly hold you back. You look and feel good, which is half the reason you impress almost everyone you meet.

## 17 TUESDAY *Moon Age Day 26 Moon Sign Aquarius*

You look out for the help of those you know can be of assistance today and especially people who are expert in their own particular field. Confidence is still present, though you do recognise that we can't all be good at everything. Practical jobs around the home are one area in which you might elicit support.

## 18 WEDNESDAY *Moon Age Day 27 Moon Sign Aquarius*

Discussions, particularly with loved ones, can be much more important than you might have previously thought. In one or two respects, you feel yourself to lack courage at present. The fact that you carry on, even though you might be nervous about doing so, proves that you are actually brave.

## 19 THURSDAY *Moon Age Day 28 Moon Sign Pisces*

Make as much time as possible for relaxation and don't push yourself so hard that you find it difficult to slow down your mind later. There is time to do almost anything you want, but half a dozen jobs at the same time won't help. A good day for romance – that is, if you have the time to notice that you are being observed.

## 20 FRIDAY *Moon Age Day 0 Moon Sign Pisces*

Don't expect to get all that much done today. The lunar low is inclined to get in the way and prevents you from moving forward in quite the way you might wish. If you get nervous about something you know you are going to have to say, have a little rehearsal. Even in situations where you are shaking, you can still come through.

## 21 SATURDAY *Moon Age Day 1 Moon Sign Aries*

There are a few possible gains to be made today, some of which come as a surprise. This means you have to be ready for almost anything. Powers of communication are good at present and you can really make an impression when it counts the most. Don't be too quick to judge the wisdom of friends.

## 22 SUNDAY *Moon Age Day 2 Moon Sign Aries*

Some delays in favoured projects are inevitable now, which is why you have to exercise a little patience, particularly at the beginning of next week. Don't rush into anything, but use that capable Virgo brain and think things through carefully. A little preparation is worthwhile in any job you undertake today.

## 23 MONDAY *Moon Age Day 3 Moon Sign Taurus*

There are planetary aspects around now that favour a slightly rasher approach, particularly in terms of love and romance. You need to speak your mind, especially to your partner, and particularly when you have something good to say. Nobody is going to be in the least embarrassed by your behaviour now, but it is unusual for you.

## 24 TUESDAY *Moon Age Day 4 Moon Sign Taurus*

Don't be too quick to jump to conclusions. There probably isn't too much time for thinking in any case. This is potentially a day of social happenings, and a period when you will not want to be tied down by too many routines. Of special concern now could be your garden, or perhaps other places far from your abode.

## 25 WEDNESDAY *Moon Age Day 5 Moon Sign Gemini*

If you find yourself facing some sort of social engagement, it would be best to prepare yourself fully first. Although you are a good public speaker, there is a slightly shy side to your nature on occasions and you have to overcome this now. Try not to fuss too much about details, as this is one of the less than perfect traits of your sign.

## 26 THURSDAY *Moon Age Day 6 Moon Sign Gemini*

Avoid getting involved in arguments today. Not only are most of them completely unnecessary, but also you don't stand much chance of winning out. Even if you feel you have scored a victory, it will be marginal, to say the least. You don't actually have to agree with everyone, but neither do you have to disagree deliberately.

## 27 FRIDAY *Moon Age Day 7 Moon Sign Cancer*

As the working week draws to a close, there could well be a few tasks that have been left undone. You need to deal with these, if you can, and clear the decks for further action after the weekend. It is also important to make sure you won't have to worry about practical or professional issues across the next couple of days.

## 28 SATURDAY *Moon Age Day 8 Moon Sign Cancer*

Give yourself a little time to become acclimatised to change, no matter how necessary it seems to be right now. The most difficult situation for Virgo people right at the moment would be to contemplate a house move. Even reorganising the furniture is something you will want to think long and hard about.

## 29 SUNDAY *Moon Age Day 9 Moon Sign Cancer*

The practical side of your nature is very much in evidence, but unless you are really sure about what you are doing, leave it until later. This Sunday is best for planning, and for observing the way others do things. You need these periods of calm and quiet, in order to deal with the busier times that crop up regularly this year.

## 30 MONDAY *Moon Age Day 10 Moon Sign Leo*

Things might quieten down somewhat today and tomorrow, but that doesn't mean you fail to take notice of what is going on around you. On the contrary, you really are keeping your eyes open and details that others don't see are immediately obvious to you. Don't be too rash with money right now.

## 31 TUESDAY *Moon Age Day 11 Moon Sign Leo*

In terms of communications at least, this is likely to be a hectic but enjoyable sort of day. You can afford to back your hunches to a great extent and you won't be holding back when it comes to ideas. Friends ought to prove very helpful and can offer some exciting alternatives on those occasions when life gets dull.

2015

## Your Month at a Glance

(+) = Opportunities are around (−) = Be on the defensive ( ) = Life is pretty ordinary

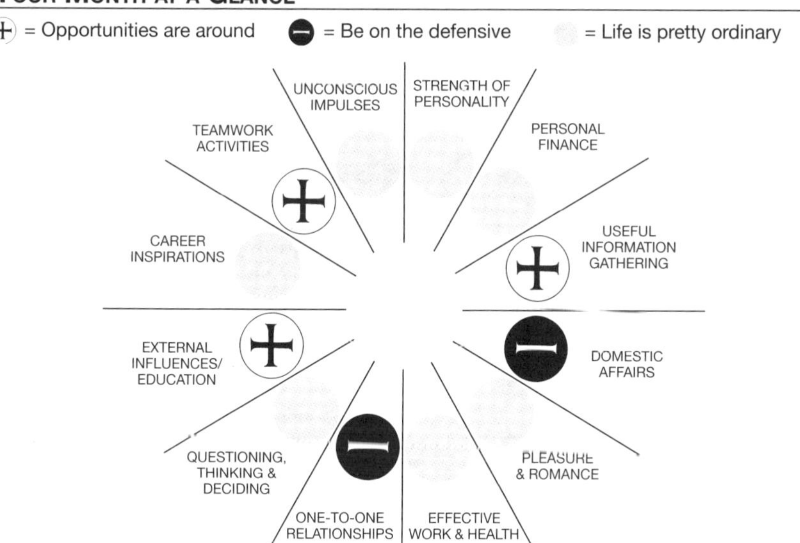


## April Highs and Lows

*Here I show you how the rhythms of the Moon will affect you this month. Like the tide, your energies and abilities will rise and fall with its pattern. When it is above the centre line, go for it, when it is below, you should be resting.*

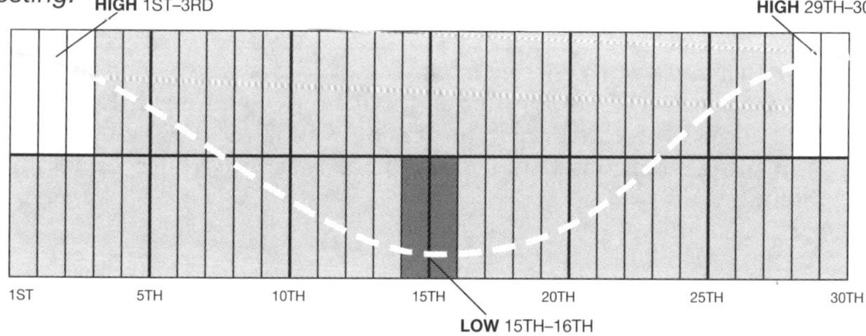

## 1 WEDNESDAY *Moon Age Day 12 Moon Sign Virgo*

**Certain situations can seem fairly chaotic today, particularly in terms of necessary communication. Actually, you will probably be far better off spending some time alone and relying on your own intuition. Use caution when faced by get-rich-quick schemes. They could look too good to be true and probably are.**

## 2 THURSDAY *Moon Age Day 13 Moon Sign Virgo*

**Speak your mind today, and expect everyone to give you their full attention. You can't have everything you want from life at present, though you can come quite close. Lady Luck is with you and it's worth investing in what you know to be a good idea, especially if you thought it up for yourself.**

## 3 FRIDAY *Moon Age Day 14 Moon Sign Virgo*

**You are probably being very co-operative in money matters today, which can pay dividends later on. Affairs of the heart should be progressing in a satisfactory manner, and as the day advances the benefits of the lunar high show themselves more and more. Keep a high profile in social situations.**

## 4 SATURDAY *Moon Age Day 15 Moon Sign Libra*

Personal relationships can be a great deal of help today when it comes to financial support and future planning of a practical nature. Casual conversations lead to ideas that can prove to be both interesting and useful. Look out for unusual happenings that start you thinking along unconventional lines.

## 5 SUNDAY *Moon Age Day 16 Moon Sign Libra*

Valuable information is coming your way, but don't take anything at face value. Remain determined to follow your own appointed course in life. Routines can be a bit of a bind, so it helps to vary your routines considerably.

## 6 MONDAY *Moon Age Day 17 Moon Sign Scorpio*

It appears that you need a change from your everyday routines and the start of a new working week could offer all the incentive you need. Keep active and don't allow yourself to vegetate. It is only a matter of time before new and stimulating situations begin, though today is unlikely to be bristling with them.

## 7 TUESDAY

*Moon Age Day 18 Moon Sign Scorpio*

You could be so preoccupied with personal issues today that you fail to see the wood for the trees in a practical sense. In any situation, it is very important to keep your eyes on the ball. This probably isn't the best time of the month to make any major financial changes in any case. Stick with the status quo.

## 8 WEDNESDAY

*Moon Age Day 19 Moon Sign Scorpio*

Only you can decide whether to believe everything you hear today, but there could be people about who are fairly deceptive. Stay away from them if you can, but in any case use your intuition and natural Virgo caution. In matters of the heart you are being frank, outspoken and perhaps even a little brutal on occasions.

## 9 THURSDAY

*Moon Age Day 20 Moon Sign Sagittarius*

It is time to enjoy the fruits of some of your recent efforts. Financially speaking, you could be rather better off than you have been expecting and the world looks more exciting than it has for some days. Confidence to do exactly what you want is never far away. All in all, you should be looking and feeling good.

## 10 FRIDAY

*Moon Age Day 21 Moon Sign Sagittarius*

You are unlikely to have the time for personal indulgences today and will probably be tied up with one issue or another for most of the time. If you can break away, do your best to foster some personal desire or aspiration. The more you feel you are moving forward, the greater the incentive for a positive period.

## 11 SATURDAY

*Moon Age Day 22 Moon Sign Capricorn*

A rather pressing domestic matter could arise today. Take it in your stride and don't necessarily think that you have to find answers here and now. There are certain issues that would be best left on the back burner for the moment, leaving you to have fun and to take a more general look at life.

## 12 SUNDAY

*Moon Age Day 23 Moon Sign Capricorn*

It does appear that material issues are uppermost in your mind at present and you need to face some of these head on early in the day. If you are at work today, you are positive and aspirational, though it is in terms of love and romance that you tend to have the best of all worlds right now.

## 13 MONDAY *Moon Age Day 24 Moon Sign Aquarius*

Achieving a good balance between self-interest and the need the world has of you will not be too difficult today. Although you are still very committed to change, you can also see just how important it would be to think carefully before you act. Today the world at large registers a very sensible Virgo subject.

## 14 TUESDAY *Moon Age Day 25 Moon Sign Aquarius*

There is a chance today to broaden your personal horizons and to get on side with issues that might have puzzled you previously. Friendship is strong and people who have not played an important part in your life up to now start to become more significant. Look out for some unexpected financial gains.

## 15 WEDNESDAY *Moon Age Day 26 Moon Sign Pisces*

It could seem as if you do nothing but wait today. Not to worry, the lunar low is around in any case, so you won't be able to move any mountains. You have time to think and the ability to structure your thoughts into patterns of behaviour that will be far more appropriate on another day.

## 16 THURSDAY *Moon Age Day 27 Moon Sign Pisces*

The lunar low is likely to bring unexpected obstacles today. However, you are able to make the best of them and if you rely on people you know to have natural good luck, you can overcome some difficulties. On a personal level, this is a day that ought to prove both interesting and stimulating.

## 17 FRIDAY *Moon Age Day 28 Moon Sign Aries*

Make this a good day for new input and ideas, some of which can really bring gains into your life in the fullness of time. There are some fairly unusual circumstances about, leading to many coincidences and strange happenings. Most of these seem geared towards your greater success.

## 18 SATURDAY *Moon Age Day 29 Moon Sign Aries*

You can't avoid the feeling that this is a time in your life for off with the old and on with the new. That's fine, but don't go too far just because you are on a roll. It is just possible that you could abandon ways of thinking and acting that are not at all redundant in favour of ones that don't serve you as well.

## 19 SUNDAY

*Moon Age Day 0 Moon Sign Taurus*

Impressive socially, you find the world presenting you with enjoyable and stimulating company. Take life in your stride and you should enjoy today and can particularly make a great deal of personal offers and invitations. When it comes to romance, you are in a good position to show your lover exactly how you feel.

## 20 MONDAY

*Moon Age Day 1 Moon Sign Taurus*

A slightly less interesting period might seem to be in evidence, following the generally positive trends of yesterday. At work it would be sensible to avoid putting off until tomorrow what you can easily do today, so focus on the tasks at hand. People you haven't met for ages are likely to make a return to your life now.

## 21 TUESDAY

*Moon Age Day 2 Moon Sign Gemini*

Where emotional ties are concerned, you need to be rather more careful than usual. It is easy for others to misunderstand what you are saying and to come to the wrong conclusions as a result. There are gains to be made through inventiveness and by being in the right place at the most advantageous time.

## 22 WEDNESDAY

*Moon Age Day 3 Moon Sign Gemini*

There is now much to be gained from widening your personal horizons. Young Virgo subjects or those looking for love can expect opportunities to come along. Maybe you have an admirer you would never have guessed at, or perhaps you discover that a friend wishes to be very much more.

## 23 THURSDAY

*Moon Age Day 4 Moon Sign Gemini*

You can be streets ahead of others at work or in any competitive endeavour. Don't fight shy of letting people know what you think. It is true that you are rather outspoken at the moment, but much of what you have to say makes a great deal of sense. Keep a sense of proportion regarding spending.

## 24 FRIDAY

*Moon Age Day 5 Moon Sign Cancer*

Now that the Sun is in your solar ninth house, you can expect a new phase to begin, during which the real you begins to show. Intellectual pursuits are emphasised and your mind is working well. Now you can address problems that might have taxed you in earlier weeks or months.

## 25 SATURDAY *Moon Age Day 6 Moon Sign Cancer*

The potential for making smooth progress is strong. At work, you should be able to address most matters well and are unlikely to back down over issues you see as being important. Your personal life is likely to be settled, with romantic interludes permeating a generally sedate period.

## 26 SUNDAY *Moon Age Day 7 Moon Sign Leo*

When it comes to general initiative, you won't be found in any way wanting on this Sunday. At the same time, you need to take a close look around you. The summer is approaching fast, with the nights getting shorter and everything in the garden beginning to grow. Like the flowers, you need more space now.

## 27 MONDAY *Moon Age Day 8 Moon Sign Leo*

Professional matters seem to be on a very definite roll, making you increasingly confident about situations, a fact that shows in the way you deal with them. Don't be too quick to make widespread changes to domestic arrangements, at least without bearing in mind the opinions of family members.

## 28 TUESDAY *Moon Age Day 9 Moon Sign Leo*

The dynamo to get things done in a practical sense is strong, reconfirming your belief that you are doing the right things at the right time. Congratulations may be in order somewhere in the family or amongst your dearest friends. You will be the first to make a fuss of the people concerned and to show your joy.

## 29 WEDNESDAY *Moon Age Day 10 Moon Sign Virgo*

**This would be a good time to exploit a potentially lucky period. Success now doesn't really depend on gambling, but you will be inclined to back your own hunches and to make it plain to others that you know your own business best. Confident and quite dynamic, the world is going to take notice of you now.**

## 30 THURSDAY *Moon Age Day 11 Moon Sign Virgo*

**This is another excellent time for putting your luck to the test. Progressive decision-making is also possible, together with a strong sense of destiny regarding specific issues. Elements of the past have a bearing on the present and there may be a significant number of coincidences cropping up now.**

# May

2015

## Your Month at a Glance

+ = Opportunities are around   − = Be on the defensive   ○ = Life is pretty ordinary

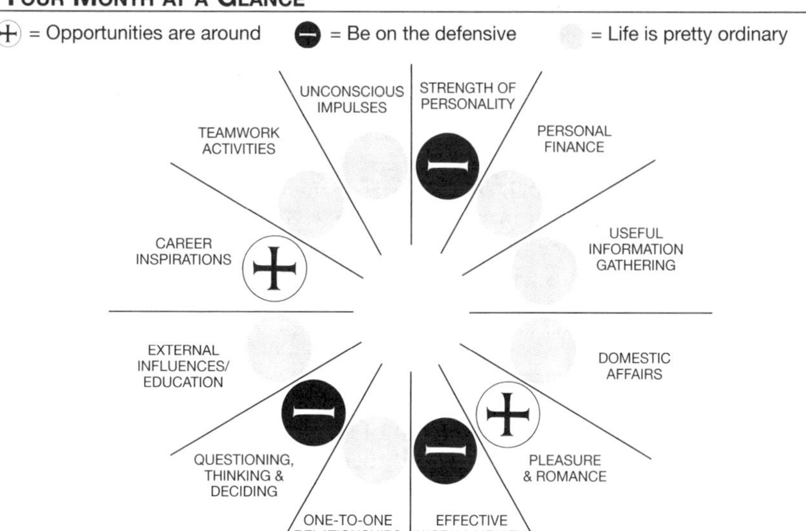


## May Highs and Lows

*Here I show you how the rhythms of the Moon will affect you this month. Like the tide, your energies and abilities will rise and fall with its pattern. When it is above the centre line, go for it, when it is below, you should be resting.*

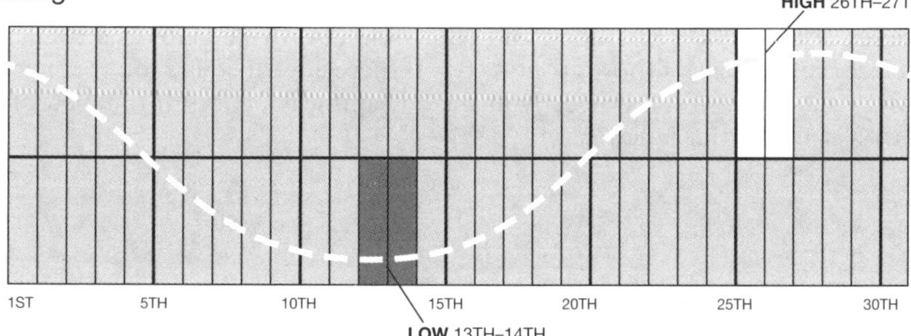

## 1 FRIDAY
*Moon Age Day 12 Moon Sign Libra*

Certain discussions in the wider world could have an argumentative side to them, something you will probably want to avoid. Although you wish to put your point of view across, there isn't much point in making enemies on the way. Your gentler approach works better, so defuse situations when you can.

## 2 SATURDAY
*Moon Age Day 13 Moon Sign Libra*

Present trends do not present the most positive circumstances for flexing your intellect. Some of your decision-making is a little rusty and you will have to spend time thinking things through. Keep an open mind about changes in and around your home, perhaps leaving some of them until later.

## 3 SUNDAY
*Moon Age Day 14 Moon Sign Libra*

You ought to be able to latch on to better financial trends that come along any time now. This is not an area of life that you will be thinking about exclusively, but it does need attention. Friends may prove to be demanding, but what they give back is worth any amount of effort on your part today.

## 4 MONDAY
*Moon Age Day 15 Moon Sign Scorpio*

There are signs that there could be financial or professional gains to be made today. This could be an ideal time to start new projects, particularly at work. When the responsibilities are out of the way, you should think about having fun. Mix and match today, with periods of high activity and other times of relaxation.

## 5 TUESDAY
*Moon Age Day 16 Moon Sign Scorpio*

Power challenges are likely today, but you have a unique way of dealing with them. Flying off the handle certainly isn't your way now and wouldn't work too well in any case. Slow and steady wins the race. Your gentle and considered approach, backed by Virgo strength, is all you need.

## 6 WEDNESDAY
*Moon Age Day 17 Moon Sign Sagittarius*

Energy levels could peak today, and you could also make gains as a result of the very real efforts of those around you. If there is a particular job that needs doing, get it out of the way early in the day and leave yourself time later for whatever takes your fancy.

## 7 THURSDAY *Moon Age Day 18 Moon Sign Sagittarius*

The pace of life continues to be fairly fast and issues related to communication now arise all the time. There is barely time to stop and take a breath, unless, of course, you make a determined decision to slow things down. There are friends and even colleagues who are in a good position to lend a hand.

## 8 FRIDAY *Moon Age Day 19 Moon Sign Capricorn*

Change and diversity are the legacies of today's planetary influences. Staying at home and sticking with routine probably won't suit you at all. On the contrary, you prefer to be out and about, mixing with the people you like to be with. By the evening, you can really put your social hat on.

## 9 SATURDAY *Moon Age Day 20 Moon Sign Capricorn*

You can enjoy all sorts of banter and even a few low-key rows today, which has not recently been your way at all. Certainly the more contentious qualities of your nature are showing and you will stick up for yourself, sometimes when you are not even being attacked. Personal attachments are untouched by these trends.

## 10 SUNDAY *Moon Age Day 21 Moon Sign Aquarius*

Take advantage of planetary trends highlighting progress in areas of life that could have been ignored of late. Comfort and security also make an appearance, particularly later in the day. Look out for more solid financial possibilities.

## 11 MONDAY *Moon Age Day 22 Moon Sign Aquarius*

This looks like a good period for all domestic matters, although you will not be ignoring personal attachments, which are at the forefront of your mind at this time. This is a day for pacing yourself and bringing others round to your point of view, using nothing more than gentle persuasion.

## 12 TUESDAY *Moon Age Day 23 Moon Sign Aquarius*

Today should find you in a mellow frame of mind and particularly drawn towards people born under the air signs of Gemini, Libra and especially Aquarius. These are generally lively types, which suits that particular aspect of your present nature. Stand by your decisions at work, even if others disagree.

## 13 WEDNESDAY *Moon Age Day 24 Moon Sign Pisces*

When it comes to obligations, you might want to take life rather easily at present. The lunar low makes you somewhat lethargic and less than happy to push yourself physically. Routines suit you at the moment, because there is great security in doing what you know and understand.

## 14 THURSDAY *Moon Age Day 25 Moon Sign Pisces*

Avoid disappointments by not allowing yourself to get in positions that could prove awkward. There might be periods of relative silence today, but if so they tend to be chosen rather than thrust upon you. Consideration for others is usually high up in your priorities and there is no reason to believe that today is any different.

## 15 FRIDAY *Moon Age Day 26 Moon Sign Aries*

With great enthusiasm for new ideas and the chance to make a particular sort of progress, today offers variety and plenty of determination. What you show to the world is the best of Virgo, whilst at the same time retaining a sort of mystique that specific individuals find totally compelling.

## 16 SATURDAY *Moon Age Day 27 Moon Sign Aries*

Your affable nature is on display for the weekend. As a result, you should enjoy great popularity, especially when in the company of people you think a great deal about. Don't be in the least surprised if you find yourself being chatted up at some stage today. The social and friendship possibilities of the day are legion.

## 17 SUNDAY *Moon Age Day 28 Moon Sign Taurus*

You may have to move about a little today in order to find the degree of happiness you seek. Wanderlust is part of what this weekend is about and the time of year is right for you to be spending more time out of doors. You love nature, and being in its presence is certainly good for you at a spiritual level.

## 18 MONDAY *Moon Age Day 0 Moon Sign Taurus*

You could find this to be a rather taxing time at work, leading you to be grateful once the responsibility is out of the way and you can finally please yourself. Socially speaking, you are on top form, which maybe one of the reasons you are less professionally inclined just at the moment.

## 19 TUESDAY ☿ *Moon Age Day 1 Moon Sign Gemini*

This is one of the best days of this month to enjoy what personal freedom surrounds you now. In some ways you could feel hemmed in by circumstances and will be keen to break down barriers as much as possible. Stay mobile and give your full attention to any situation that stimulates your mind.

## 20 WEDNESDAY ☿ *Moon Age Day 2 Moon Sign Gemini*

Love life and romantic matters show a definite improvement with the arrival of the midweek period. This may be partly due to the fact that you have more time to concentrate on the needs of those around you, and particularly your partner. Jobs are quick to mount up at home, but don't be too quick to volunteer.

## 21 THURSDAY ☿ *Moon Age Day 3 Moon Sign Cancer*

In social matters especially, the impact of your personality is extremely strong at present. Do what you can to make a favourable impression, particularly amongst people who you know are on your side. There are some revolutionary ideas about at present and you are not shy about promoting them.

## 22 FRIDAY ☿ *Moon Age Day 4 Moon Sign Cancer*

Loved ones offer a definite dose of reassurance today, together with an ability to lift your spirits across the upcoming weekend. Friends, too, are important to have around and one or two of them have interesting things to tell you. Where money is concerned, it is better to save than spend at the moment.

## 23 SATURDAY ☿ *Moon Age Day 5 Moon Sign Leo*

Standard responses don't work too well with some folk now and you might have to be rather ruthless if you want to get your message across. You don't exactly have to be cruel but when you know you are working towards someone's good, you can afford to go to town a little. Beware of minor family upsets.

## 24 SUNDAY ☿ *Moon Age Day 6 Moon Sign Leo*

There can be some shortcuts to success today. This is unusual for Virgo, which is used to working hard for most of what it gets. Review all situations carefully and also look out for a real bargain, because they, too, are appearing at the moment. Generally speaking, things are on the up.

## 25 MONDAY ☿ *Moon Age Day 7 Moon Sign Leo*

Your powers of leadership are definitely increasing. The Sun is now in your solar tenth house, which is a confidence booster of the most positive sort. Contributing to the happiness that others feel from life is also part of the gift you bring at present and moving about generally appeals to you.

## 26 TUESDAY ☿ *Moon Age Day 8 Moon Sign Virgo*

**Striking personal successes become possible today, as the Moon moves into your zodiac sign. Go for what you want with all guns blazing, though without upsetting anyone else on the way. Your nature is now very progressive and you should be filled with good ideas that are also practical ones.**

## 27 WEDNESDAY ☿ *Moon Age Day 9 Moon Sign Virgo*

**This would be an excellent time to approach people who definitely have influence on your life. You could be taking on new projects and generally finding ways to make life more successful and, of course, comfortable. Your nature is bright and alert, leading to even greater popularity.**

## 28 THURSDAY ☿ *Moon Age Day 10 Moon Sign Libra*

Social high spots are evident at the start of today, with no desire on your part to stick around the house and vegetate. You would rather be climbing a high hill, or maybe looking out at a blue sea. All in all, this would not be at all a bad time to think about taking a holiday.

## 29 FRIDAY ☿ *Moon Age Day 11 Moon Sign Libra*

Your personality begins to shine out and is most obvious in the way you are happy to talk to anyone about almost any topic. So noisy are you at present that it will be difficult for others to get a word in edgeways. It is unlikely that they will object because you are so good to have around now.

## 30 SATURDAY ☿ *Moon Age Day 12 Moon Sign Libra*

Although your mind is potentially geared towards your job today, many Virgo people will not even be at work. Instead, you need to think about movement, of every conceivable kind. Sedentary pursuits won't appeal to you at all because you only want to be moving wherever the will takes you.

## 31 SUNDAY ☿ *Moon Age Day 13 Moon Sign Scorpio*

Take advantage of circumstances that are clearly working in your favour. Although there are some slight obstacles to be overcome, the horizon today does look a good deal clearer than might have been the case for some of you earlier. Friends prove to be extremely helpful, at a time when it matters the most.

# June

2015

## Your Month at a Glance

(+) = Opportunities are around (−) = Be on the defensive ( ) = Life is pretty ordinary

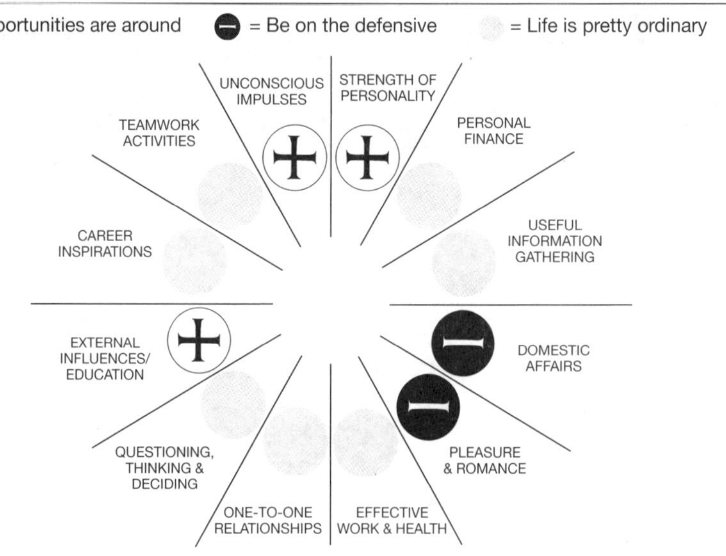


## June Highs and Lows

*Here I show you how the rhythms of the Moon will affect you this month. Like the tide, your energies and abilities will rise and fall with its pattern. When it is above the centre line, go for it, when it is below, you should be resting.*

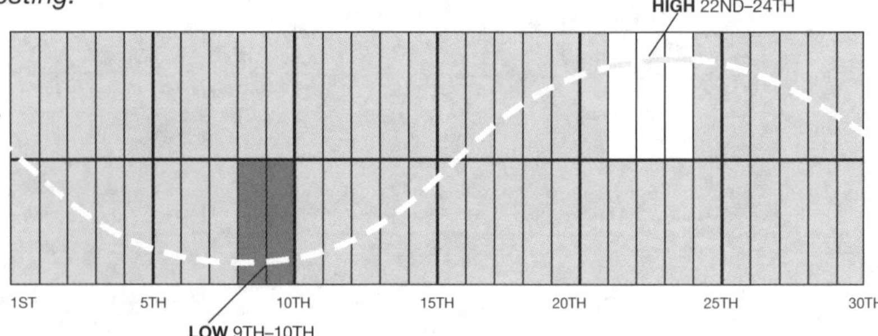

## 1 MONDAY ☿ *Moon Age Day 14 Moon Sign Scorpio*

It is your professional life that continues to be most rewarding at present. Good news is likely to be on the way that might also have a bearing on your romantic interests. Hold tight to money for the moment, because the best bargains come along later this month. In the meantime, practise care over spending.

## 2 TUESDAY ☿ *Moon Age Day 15 Moon Sign Sagittarius*

This is another day during which you should see things happening on the material plane. Finances might be favoured today, but even so try to spend your money wisely. Not everyone appears to understand your point of view, particularly regarding personal matters, but you should be able to talk them round.

## 3 WEDNESDAY ☿ *Moon Age Day 16 Moon Sign Sagittarius*

Your powers of communication are in the ascendant today and you seem to have what it takes to get your message across to others intact. If there is a particularly big task before you, the best approach today may be to nibble away at the edges of it or maybe to seek the help of a good friend.

## 4 THURSDAY ☿ *Moon Age Day 17 Moon Sign Sagittarius*

You might feel yourself more than ready to take a break, but the considerable responsibilities you face at present could make this unlikely. Conforming to expectations won't be all that easy right now and you would be better off allowing a degree of originality to enter your reasoning today.

## 5 FRIDAY ☿ *Moon Age Day 18 Moon Sign Capricorn*

There are some tensions in everyday matters that probably have to be dealt with fairly early in the day. However, don't allow these to distract you from the real job at hand, which is to promote yourself in a public forum. People really do want to hear what you have to say and you are hardly shy right now.

## 6 SATURDAY ☿ *Moon Age Day 19 Moon Sign Capricorn*

Although you could be in two minds regarding practical decisions, in the end you can rely on your common sense to tell you what to do. Do you take the advice of others or simply forge ahead under your own steam? Only you can decide. Your actions are solely dictated by logic at this time.

## 7 SUNDAY ☿ *Moon Age Day 20 Moon Sign Aquarius*

There are signs that your financial powers are looking reasonably good, even if you have to stretch cash somewhat today. Don't spend lavishly on items you don't really need and be prepared to keep an open mind about bargains. Friends are on your side, particularly in little disputes that arise now.

## 8 MONDAY ☿ *Moon Age Day 21 Moon Sign Aquarius*

Although you exhibit little in the way of self-discipline today, it doesn't seem to matter particularly. You have charm and a knowing knack of getting your own way. Even people who have seemed particularly awkward to deal with previously should be falling under your spell at some time in the near future.

## 9 TUESDAY ☿ *Moon Age Day 22 Moon Sign Pisces*

Professional progress is slowed markedly as the lunar low pays its monthly visit. Fortunately, you could take advantage of some strong planetary trends in evidence, so the power of the Moon's influence is somewhat diminished this time around. In a social and romantic sense, you may barely notice the difference.

## 10 WEDNESDAY ☿ *Moon Age Day 23 Moon Sign Pisces*

Obstacles and hold-ups of one sort or another are clearly a fact of life at the moment and there is little you can do to address or alter them. The lunar low isn't around long, but it has made you rather lethargic and less inclined to concentrate. Simply understand what is going on astrologically and all will come right.

## 11 THURSDAY ☿ *Moon Age Day 24 Moon Sign Aries*

Relationships now prove more rewarding than they might have seemed on one or two occasions recently. Close to home there are people who display their goodwill and who actively want to offer you some sort of support. This may not be needed, but it would be churlish to turn the people in question away.

## 12 FRIDAY ☿ *Moon Age Day 25 Moon Sign Aries*

Though your practical capabilities are excellent at the moment, the part of your mind used to arrange matters isn't quite so well honed. It might be necessary to check with other people and even to follow their lead in some matters. Today would be excellent for shopping and for meeting up with pals in an informal way.

## 13 SATURDAY *Moon Age Day 26 Moon Sign Taurus*

Today probably finds you dealing with frayed tempers, though almost certainly not your own. It is possible to get through far more work today than you could possibly have expected, leaving you with social moments that are snatched, but very important. Hand out some congratulations in the family.

## 14 SUNDAY *Moon Age Day 27 Moon Sign Taurus*

This would be a good period on the whole for broadening your horizons and for seeking new things to do. The Sunday can be stimulating and even exciting in a way you had not expected. You make a strong contribution to family events, but should also be able to find times to be extremely supportive of your partner or a friend.

## 15 MONDAY *Moon Age Day 28 Moon Sign Gemini*

Mind-to-mind exchanges take place today and offer you the chance to sharpen your intellect in a way that hasn't been possible for quite some time. Try to stay away from artificial stimulants of any sort right now. Your brain is managing to produce enough stimulating chemicals of its own.

## 16 TUESDAY *Moon Age Day 29 Moon Sign Gemini*

Now you can make your move, both at work and in personal situations. You look successful and impressive to the outside world, which means you are probably at the peak of your powers. Even if you don't feel entirely certain of yourself, it is the impression you give that means the most.

## 17 WEDNESDAY *Moon Age Day 0 Moon Sign Cancer*

Good news could be coming in from a number of different directions, some of which prove to be quite surprising. You will be taking this in your stride, and at the same time seeking change and diversity in your life as a whole. Don't be too surprised if you are being singled out for special treatment.

## 18 THURSDAY *Moon Age Day 1 Moon Sign Cancer*

Most matters can go your way today if you make a little effort. If there are celebrations in the family or within your friendship circle, there's a good chance you will want to join in. You have a fairly carefree attitude to life at present and can certainly enjoy all that romance offers.

## 19 FRIDAY *Moon Age Day 2 Moon Sign Cancer*

Things you learn today can be turned to your advantage, so it appears that in addition to having plenty to say yourself you are also keeping your ears open. Real power is on offer for some Virgo people, mainly in a career sense. Do as much work as you can today, because tomorrow is more about pleasure.

## 20 SATURDAY *Moon Age Day 3 Moon Sign Leo*

Another good day, and equally busy, though now much more geared towards your social life. If you wish, you can be on the go from morning until night, relishing the chance to mix with as many people as possible. Avoid family rows. You haven't caused them and don't really need to be involved at all.

## 21 SUNDAY *Moon Age Day 4 Moon Sign Leo*

Tripping the light fantastic appeals to you today. Singing, dancing, walking or swimming: whatever you do today should be active and stimulating. Getting on with others is as easy as falling off a log and you can even score some successes with folk who haven't put themselves out for you before.

## 22 MONDAY *Moon Age Day 5 Moon Sign Virgo*

**The lunar high accelerates the pace of your life and makes it hard to relax on this summer day. On the contrary, you have masses to keep you occupied and all the energy necessary to deal with what comes along. Friendship is particularly well accented later in the day.**

## 23 TUESDAY *Moon Age Day 6 Moon Sign Virgo*

**This could prove to be an excellent day to take the odd chance and stamp your own particular brand of authority on your life. Few individuals would want to stand in your way at this time and you can afford to back your hunches, probably to the hilt.**

## 24 WEDNESDAY *Moon Age Day 7 Moon Sign Virgo*

**Friendship is high on your list of priorities today, even if you are practically busy for most of the time. When you do get a moment, don't forget to say thank you for someone's kindness and bear in mind the need of people who are going through a hard time right now.**

## 25 THURSDAY *Moon Age Day 8 Moon Sign Libra*

It won't be too difficult to get your own way now, even with people who are tough nuts to crack. You are seen as being very likeable and a good deal more flexible than is sometimes the case for Virgo. Acting on impulse is not really you, but it does seem to work at present.

## 26 FRIDAY *Moon Age Day 9 Moon Sign Libra*

Career developments can be aided by people who are in the know, though you won't want to waste a second of what the day has to offer romantically and socially. You are still riding high in the estimation of most people and are especially popular with those who see you as being a source of good advice.

## 27 SATURDAY *Moon Age Day 10 Moon Sign Scorpio*

It is only if you try to do too much today that you will find yourself coming unstuck. The tried and tested Virgo route to success is especially necessary under prevailing trends. One job at a time, and every one undertaken to the very best of your ability. Slowly and surely, you achieve your objectives.

## 28 SUNDAY *Moon Age Day 11 Moon Sign Scorpio*

Although many of your personal ambitions are now clearly on course, don't overstep the mark and expect too much, either from others or yourself. You need to tread carefully where finances are concerned, and not push other people into taking financial risks that might frighten them.

## 29 MONDAY *Moon Age Day 12 Moon Sign Scorpio*

There are chores galore today, or at least that is the way it looks. Don't be too surprised if you are a little down in the dumps, though it is clear that matters lie predominantly in your own hands. Creative potential is good, but you could find obstacles being put in your path.

## 30 TUESDAY *Moon Age Day 13 Moon Sign Sagittarius*

You have a far more determined approach to problem solving now, and could actively seek out situations that you can turn to your advantage. At the same time, your nature shows a very sensitive edge, which the people you mix with the most could hardly fail to notice. You ought to be very popular around now.

2015

## Your Month at a Glance

(+) = Opportunities are around (−) = Be on the defensive ( ) = Life is pretty ordinary

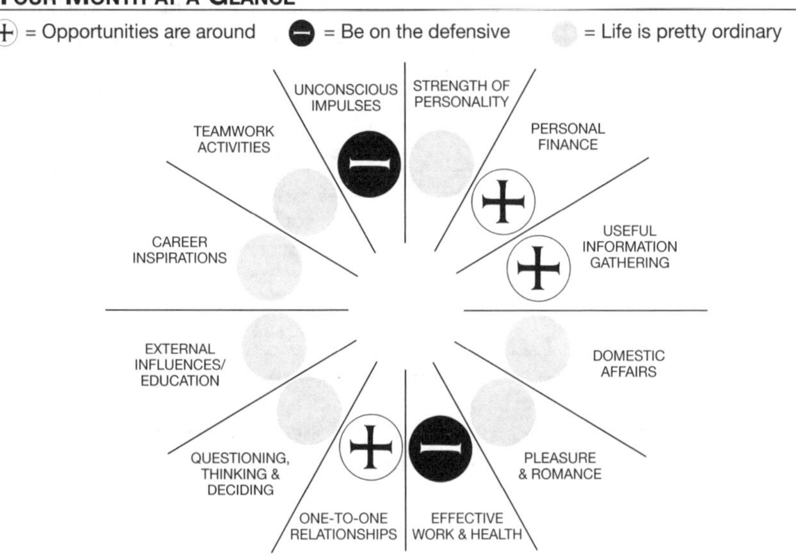


## July Highs and Lows

*Here I show you how the rhythms of the Moon will affect you this month. Like the tide, your energies and abilities will rise and fall with its pattern. When it is above the centre line, go for it, when it is below, you should be resting.*

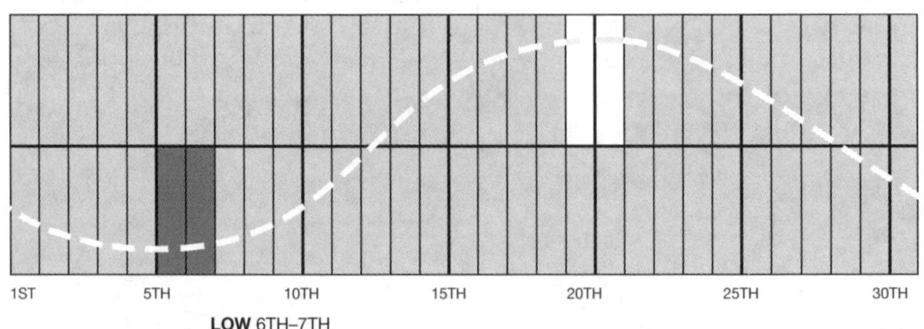

## 1 WEDNESDAY *Moon Age Day 14 Moon Sign Sagittarius*

Although you know what you want from life, you are inclined to be easily influenced today. It is important to stick to directions you have chosen for yourself previously and not to be diverted by false promises. A special friendship really begins to blossom at this time and in your spare moments you can achieve a sort of inner peace.

## 2 THURSDAY *Moon Age Day 15 Moon Sign Capricorn*

It will seem to others that you have a resolution for every problem. Things won't look quite that simple from your perspective, but as long as people have faith in your judgement, life may be somewhat easier. Don't turn down a romantic offer without thinking about it carefully.

## 3 FRIDAY *Moon Age Day 16 Moon Sign Capricorn*

With a chance of a little luck financially, you are probably going through a fairly steady sort of day in other ways. Try not to rush any fences, since it isn't remotely necessary to do so at this time. Confidence is present when you need it the most, especially in social and romantic situations.

## 4 SATURDAY *Moon Age Day 17 Moon Sign Aquarius*

You can push ahead in specific directions with sufficient confidence to tell you that you know what you are doing. Any small disappointments early in the day are likely to be swamped by much better trends that are now on the way. The people you care about the most are anxious to spend time with you now.

## 5 SUNDAY *Moon Age Day 18 Moon Sign Aquarius*

If certain pressures coming in at you from the outside seem to be too much, it is possible that you are doing more than you should. With the lunar low in view and not too much to play for in the success stakes at present, maybe you should be taking life easy and enjoying the possibilities in your personal life.

## 6 MONDAY *Moon Age Day 19 Moon Sign Pisces*

The lunar low is around. True, it doesn't have the bearing on Virgo that it does on some zodiac signs, but it can take the wind out of your sails to some extent. Adopt a matter-of-fact attitude and simply enjoy the peace and quiet that a summer day can offer. Try to relax if you can.

## 7 TUESDAY *Moon Age Day 20 Moon Sign Pisces*

A certain degree of diplomacy is called for now, maybe during a period when you are really not in the best frame of mind to offer it. Try to slow things down and take life steadily. There is nothing to be gained at all today from rushing your fences. You have tremendous staying power, but don't forget to take a rest when you need to.

## 8 WEDNESDAY *Moon Age Day 21 Moon Sign Aries*

Right now the accent is on fun and getting together with people who inspire you in some way. Although your nature is very progressive at present, you will also be going through a slightly nostalgic phase and one that is inclined to prevent you from seeing exactly what lies before you. Take lessons from the past, but little else.

## 9 THURSDAY *Moon Age Day 22 Moon Sign Aries*

You feel much easier now about making your way in the world of work. You are fairly fortunate at present, because there are plenty of people around who are willing to lend a helping hand when you need it the most. Not every situation can be addressed today however and some patience is necessary.

## 10 FRIDAY *Moon Age Day 23 Moon Sign Taurus*

A heated issue in your domestic life is inclined to surface today, probably bringing with it discussions and, in the most extreme situations, an argument. You won't really want either today, because you are seeking peace and quiet. Just as well, because this is not a good time to get on your high horse.

## 11 SATURDAY *Moon Age Day 24 Moon Sign Taurus*

Although practical matters are probably smoother than ever, there is some doubt as to personal issues. If this turns out to be the case, you can probably be sure that it is not you who is making waves. Stand by a decision you made earlier, despite the fact that others do not agree, especially younger family members.

## 12 SUNDAY *Moon Age Day 25 Moon Sign Taurus*

Trips down memory lane are fine, but they don't butter any parsnips. It is in the world of practicalities that you tend to find yourself today and there are many issues that have to be addressed. Although you remain fairly busy, there should also be more than enough time to find ways in which you can have fun.

## 13 MONDAY *Moon Age Day 26 Moon Sign Gemini*

Career developments may need more attention at the start of this working week. It could be that you are faced with certain choices or even changes. It isn't hard for you to see your way forward at present or to make the sort of decisions that will have you feeling more secure in the weeks and months to come.

## 14 TUESDAY *Moon Age Day 27 Moon Sign Gemini*

Watch out for strained relationships, even if you have not been causing the problems yourself. There are times when it is necessary to stand back and look at particular issues. You could find today to be such a period. Rules and regulations could easily get on your nerves today, so try to stay clear of them.

## 15 WEDNESDAY *Moon Age Day 28 Moon Sign Cancer*

There are good reasons why you can't expect to be number one today and disappointments are less likely if you accept this. This might be a good time for shopping, as long as spending is moderate, and you can also organise things very well, particularly in terms of working practices.

## 16 THURSDAY *Moon Age Day 0 Moon Sign Cancer*

Although opportunities to get ahead are not legion, you do recognise them well and can squeeze through any crack to get what you want. Some people might accuse you of being sneaky and self-seeking, though the truth is that you have the interests of relatives, friends and colleagues at heart.

## 17 FRIDAY *Moon Age Day 1 Moon Sign Leo*

There are certain emotional pressures that you will have to work against today. Don't be too quick to push your point of view forward, particularly when you are talking to your partner or loved ones. Confidence remains generally intact, but you can't be certain of bringing everyone on side now.

## 18 SATURDAY *Moon Age Day 2 Moon Sign Leo*

Professional and career matters could move up a notch now, even though the weekend has arrived. You might be coming to the end of a phase or task that in some ways you will be happy to leave behind. This might not be the most satisfying of days, but it does appear to bring a good deal of inner contentment.

## 19 SUNDAY *Moon Age Day 3 Moon Sign Leo*

A much more progressive and positive phase is now at hand, with the potential for advancements and a more determined attitude. People you have not mixed with for a while might be making a return to your life soon, though some of these are individuals with whom you have argued previously.

## 20 MONDAY *Moon Age Day 4 Moon Sign Virgo*

**This could be the best part of the month for actually getting things done. The lunar high brings greater confidence and allows you to influence others in ways that may not have been possible earlier. This is especially true today with regard to family members, friends and, of course, your partner.**

## 21 TUESDAY *Moon Age Day 5 Moon Sign Virgo*

**You want to cram as much in as you can at this time and since there is so much happening the social possibilities are legion. Not to worry. You know how to pace yourself, and in any case the level of energy you display right now appears to be going well off the scale.**

## 22 WEDNESDAY *Moon Age Day 6 Moon Sign Libra*

Today's influences indicate that you'd be better putting faith in your own abilities, rather than trusting to luck. It might also be a mistake to believe automatically what others are saying. You wouldn't suggest, or even believe, that people are lying. On the contrary, they might be as much in the dark as you are and merely quoting possibilities.

## 23 THURSDAY *Moon Age Day 7 Moon Sign Libra*

Along comes a socially helpful period, during which those around you are more willing than ever to put themselves out on your behalf. Don't be too quick to judge the actions or opinions of a friend, but stay flexible and even suggestible. Routines will bore you during this period, so avoid them.

## 24 FRIDAY *Moon Age Day 8 Moon Sign Libra*

Getting away from any sort of rat race appeals to you at this stage of the week. Best of all would be to have an extended weekend. Just because you are somewhat withdrawn at the moment, doesn't indicate that you are failing to come up with some startling ideas.

## 25 SATURDAY *Moon Age Day 9 Moon Sign Scorpio*

Don't let yourself be dominated by emotional impulses, particularly since many of them are not at all necessary. You need to free yourself from old habits and especially ones that you know are bad for you. With a forward-looking attitude later in the day, a greater contentment emerges.

## 26 SUNDAY *Moon Age Day 10 Moon Sign Scorpio*

Despite a more progressive phase yesterday, the general trend is still quieter than usual. You can blame this on the position of the Sun, which now occupies your solar twelfth house. At least from that position it encourages you to be more intuitive, and to think things through in an almost meticulous manner.

## 27 MONDAY *Moon Age Day 11 Moon Sign Sagittarius*

Things are looking promising and you will almost certainly find yourself in very enjoyable company at the moment. There are gains to be made on the financial scene and also possibly at work. What pleases you the most, however, is that you feel more confident and better able to co-operate with others.

## 28 TUESDAY *Moon Age Day 12 Moon Sign Sagittarius*

Don't be afraid to consider specific changes to your life, if you know in your heart that they are going to benefit you later. Not everything goes your way today, but enjoy the summer and make the most of every opportunity to find fresh fields and pastures new.

## 29 WEDNESDAY *Moon Age Day 13 Moon Sign Capricorn*

Life looks good and you could find today that group activities begin to work well for you. Creative potential is good and growth in certain areas of your life seems almost organic. Getting on side with people who have been awkward previously is much easier than you might have expected.

## 30 THURSDAY *Moon Age Day 14 Moon Sign Capricorn*

It would be best to opt for some light relief today and that is what you should be thinking about. There are substantial gains to be made where friendship is concerned, and sociable associations with others could also lead to you discovering ways to get ahead in a financial as well as a personal way.

## 31 FRIDAY

*Moon Age Day 15 Moon Sign Aquarius*

There is good assistance for practical projects today, as long as you are willing to go out and look for it. It is quite likely that some of your present ideas have a good ability to bear fruit, though unless you seek some help you may never know. There is the potential for romance to throw up surprises now.

2015

## Your Month at a Glance

(+) = Opportunities are around (−) = Be on the defensive (○) = Life is pretty ordinary

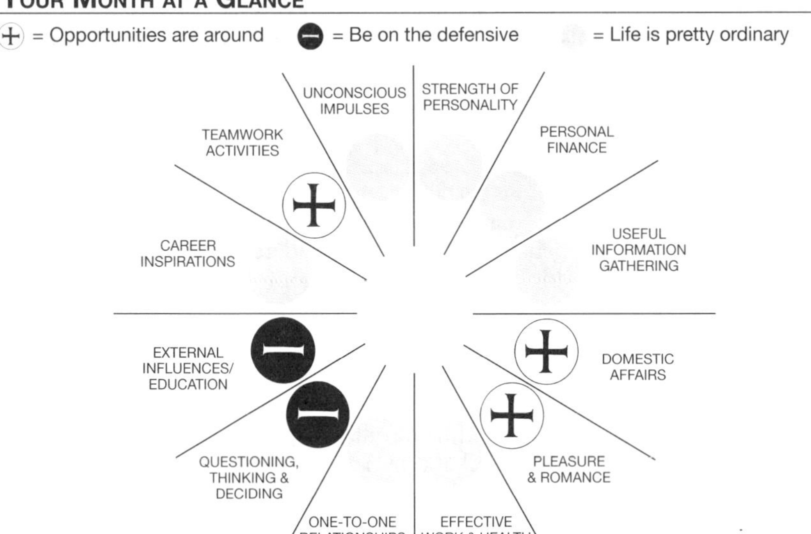


## August Highs and Lows

*Here I show you how the rhythms of the Moon will affect you this month. Like the tide, your energies and abilities will rise and fall with its pattern. When it is above the centre line, go for it, when it is below, you should be resting.*

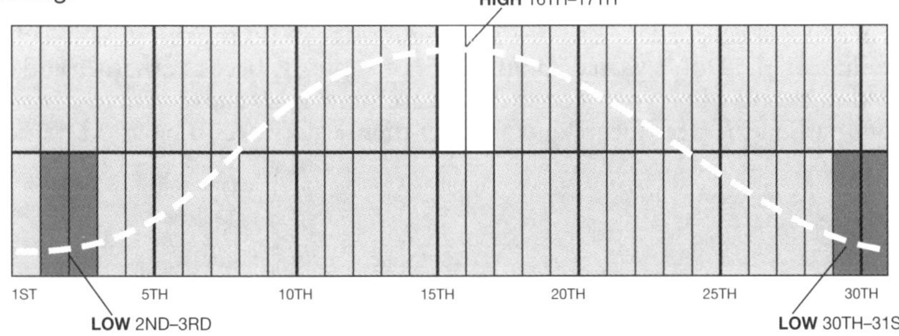

## 1 SATURDAY *Moon Age Day 16 Moon Sign Aquarius*

Avoid getting carried away with schemes that quite frankly don't have all that much chance of working to your advantage. There are gains to be made today, though these are not all that likely to be financial in nature. Relationships look good, as do all social and sporting efforts on your part today.

## 2 SUNDAY *Moon Age Day 17 Moon Sign Pisces*

This is not a day during which significant progress is likely to be made. As a result, you need to consolidate and to wait patiently for matters to mature. In the meantime, do your best to enjoy yourself and spend more time doing those things that feel right in a social and personal sense.

## 3 MONDAY *Moon Age Day 18 Moon Sign Pisces*

The art of good conversation is certainly not dead as far as you are concerned. Start the week by chatting to anyone who will listen, and be prepared to be singled out to speak on behalf of others. Your leadership skills are now being recognised, even if you don't consider you have any.

## 4 TUESDAY *Moon Age Day 19 Moon Sign Aries*

It might be evident that hearth and home is the place you want to be and that you are not all that keen to be out and about too much today. This may be a good thing. Dashing around from pillar to post for days on end is not really what your zodiac sign is all about. You are, however, very purposeful when at work.

## 5 WEDNESDAY *Moon Age Day 20 Moon Sign Aries*

There ought to be plenty of high spirits attending most of your activities today. You see yourself in a positive light right now and will be doing all you can to make other people happy, too. There are also signs that you could be introduced to an admirer you didn't know you had.

## 6 THURSDAY *Moon Age Day 21 Moon Sign Aries*

It may now be a challenge to be in the right place to do the things you feel to be important. Don't worry about a lack of support, because that should be around as and when you need it. There are some interesting people crossing your path in the near future and a few of them will prove to be good friends.

## 7 FRIDAY *Moon Age Day 22 Moon Sign Taurus*

In a social sense, you appear to be getting along well at the moment. It's true that there will be certain people around you don't care for, but that is always going to be the case. Close friends might prove to be particularly attentive at this time and they offer you insights that will prove to be very important.

## 8 SATURDAY *Moon Age Day 23 Moon Sign Taurus*

You won't appeal to everyone at the moment. Once again, it has to be said that this is always going to be the case, no matter how you feel about the situation. Most of the time you are fair and kind, but there are a few people in the world who won't be pleased, no matter what you do. Try a change of tack at work.

## 9 SUNDAY *Moon Age Day 24 Moon Sign Gemini*

Although it could appear right now that the grass is greener on the other side of just about any fence, this isn't the case at all. Simply plod along and enjoy the gains that those around you are making. This is your chance to recharge flagging batteries, because by tomorrow you will be well up to speed.

## 10 MONDAY *Moon Age Day 25 Moon Sign Gemini*

Now you are in a position to make a bigger impression on others. With your energy levels pretty high and in possession of a great deal of charm, the time has come to ask for what you want. If you feel you are being unfairly treated in some way, today is a fine time to make your feelings known.

## 11 TUESDAY *Moon Age Day 26 Moon Sign Cancer*

Try to get away somewhere around about this time. Even if you don't have a holiday planned, a shorter change of scene would do you the world of good. What you definitely don't need at this time of year is to be stuck indoors, with no view of nature and no gentle breeze blowing across your face.

## 12 WEDNESDAY *Moon Age Day 27 Moon Sign Cancer*

Stand by for a few disagreements caused by misunderstandings as much as anything. The way to avoid arguments is to talk matters through carefully and freely. Although you feel quite passionate about specific matters, it might be best not to push the point home too hard. Instead, seek a peaceful middle to the week.

## 13 THURSDAY *Moon Age Day 28 Moon Sign Leo*

With plenty of incentives, a supercharged ego begins to emerge. Although it isn't your way to sing your praises to the sky, you could well be doing so now. Your strength lies in your confidence in almost any situation. You look particularly good on the social front and when faced with romantic proposals.

## 14 FRIDAY *Moon Age Day 29 Moon Sign Leo*

This is a good day for finance, which could bring you to a sense of satisfaction in your life that might have been missing somewhat of late. There are opportunities to speak your mind in a romantic sense and so some excitement is on the cards. Find interesting things to do today in the company of happy people.

## 15 SATURDAY *Moon Age Day 0 Moon Sign Leo*

You may decide to wind down certain activities, at least for the moment. If you are feeling a little lacklustre today, you will feel happier to let someone else take the strain. Some great chances are not too far away and it is likely that you will actively want to plan ahead of them. That requires time to think.

## 16 SUNDAY *Moon Age Day 1 Moon Sign Virgo*

**Decisions you make at the moment tend to be quite lucky, a situation for which you can thank the lunar high. It's time to go for gold and to trust in your own judgement, which tends to be very sound now. Travel could be possible, with holidays beckoning or perhaps trips arranged at short notice.**

## 17 MONDAY *Moon Age Day 2 Moon Sign Virgo*

**As was the case yesterday, you can get your own way and make life work out more or less the way you would wish. Give yourself a pat on the back for something you have just achieved, but don't allow the situation to go to your head. There is plenty more to do, and right now you have the energy to move mountains.**

## 18 TUESDAY *Moon Age Day 3 Moon Sign Libra*

You show yourself as having a great deal of charm today, which is why you can be cheeky and get away with all sorts. Don't forget to keep in touch with family members who might be at a distance, and also friends you haven't seen for quite some time.

## 19 WEDNESDAY *Moon Age Day 4 Moon Sign Libra*

It appears that you are willing to stimulate the competitive instincts that you naturally possess. People can't get away with trying to fool you, and it is possible that you also take well to puzzles of almost any sort today. Once again, you feel the need to get out into the warm, summer air.

## 20 THURSDAY *Moon Age Day 5 Moon Sign Libra*

You now enjoy the company of a whole host of different sorts of people. Be willing to spend time with unusual types who have a very different view of life from the one you generally hold. Don't get involved in family rows. You won't be starting them and haven't a great deal to contribute.

## 21 FRIDAY *Moon Age Day 6 Moon Sign Scorpio*

There is a warning around that today could be slightly difficult emotionally. You need to be absolutely sure that you understand what others are saying, particularly your partner. As long as you are willing to talk things through steadily, all should be well. Make sure you have all the facts, rather than flying off the handle.

## 22 SATURDAY *Moon Age Day 7 Moon Sign Scorpio*

Progress with material matters could be slow today, but never mind. Instead of worrying too much about money, turn your mind in the direction of personal attachments, which can offer a great deal. You could choose to retreat into routines if you feel threatened.

## 23 SUNDAY *Moon Age Day 8 Moon Sign Sagittarius*

Strengths emerge again, possibly with more force than has been the case at any time for weeks. You are showing the positive traits of a typical Virgo subject now. This means you can write and speak well, and best of all, you have genuine command. People won't argue with your decisions right now.

## 24 MONDAY *Moon Age Day 9 Moon Sign Sagittarius*

Your versatility is what counts at the moment. You can turn your hand to almost anything, and what is more you enjoy yourself whilst you are at it. Trends continue to suggest that a holiday or even a short break could be very enjoyable. Keep plugging away with regard to objectives you know to be important.

## 25 TUESDAY *Moon Age Day 10 Moon Sign Sagittarius*

Your ego is boosted tremendously at what could turn out to be one of the most progressive phases for the whole of August. Be certain of what you want from life and then decide how to get it. Since there are so many people around who want to help you out, there is little chance of failure.

## 26 WEDNESDAY *Moon Age Day 11 Moon Sign Capricorn*

If you've been waiting for information for a long time, you could still be in the dark. Take things steadily in a professional sense, but don't be afraid to paint the town red once work is out of the way. Any form of outdoor activity suits you down to the ground during this week.

## 27 THURSDAY *Moon Age Day 12 Moon Sign Capricorn*

Friendly co-operation is what sets today apart. You can make gains through patience and perseverance and by being in the right place at the best possible time. Intuition works strongly, leading you to all sorts of conclusions that might astound others. Variety is now the spice of your social life.

## 28 FRIDAY *Moon Age Day 13 Moon Sign Aquarius*

When it comes to sorting out everyday matters, you attitude might be at fault today. There are some tasks you simply don't want to undertake, it's as simple as that. Trying to get a Virgo subject to do anything that goes against the grain is more or less impossible. Your stubborn streak is showing.

## 29 SATURDAY *Moon Age Day 14 Moon Sign Aquarius*

Close emotional attachments work better for you today than casual friendships or even associations at work. It might not be all that easy to see your way forward, particularly in a financial sense, but there are always people around who will offer sound advice and a helping hand.

## 30 SUNDAY *Moon Age Day 15 Moon Sign Pisces*

Although your mind today might be almost anywhere except on the task at hand, there is a dreamy sort of quality to your thinking that feels very seductive. You can get things done if you enrol the support of people within your family, or maybe friends. Subconsciously, you are on the verge of a breakthrough.

## 31 MONDAY

*Moon Age Day 16 Moon Sign Pisces*

If you are willing to take a back seat away from the action, you could look at matters in a very different light today. An occasional enforced absence from the mainstream doesn't do you any harm at all. On the contrary, it makes it possible for you to look at routine situations in a revolutionary way.

## Your Month at a Glance

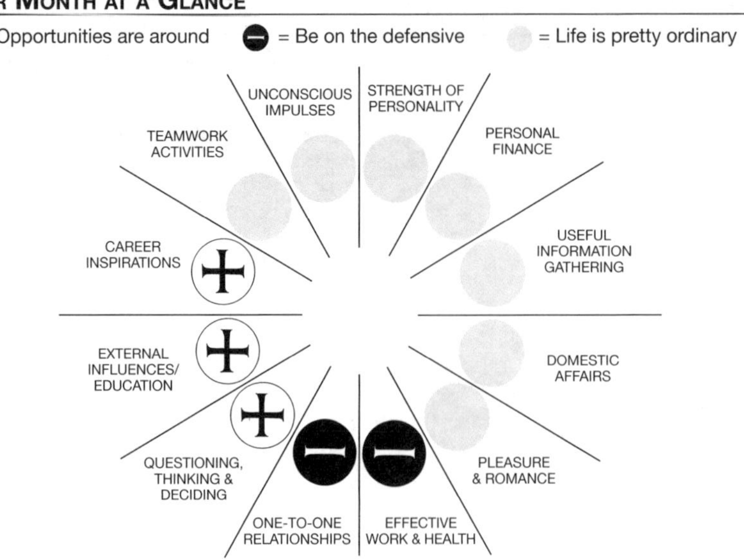


## September Highs and Lows

*Here I show you how the rhythms of the Moon will affect you this month. Like the tide, your energies and abilities will rise and fall with its pattern. When it is above the centre line, go for it, when it is below, you should be resting.*

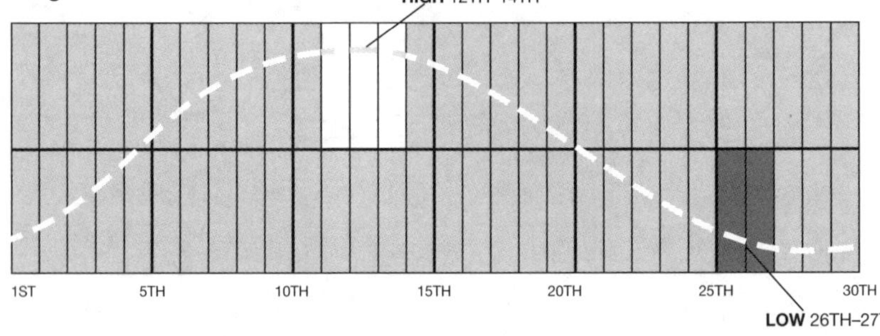

## 1 TUESDAY

*Moon Age Day 17 Moon Sign Aries*

Most of your truly rewarding moments today are likely to come through associations with house and home. People show you how fond they are of you and might be offering to help you in tangible ways. Stay away from controversy at work and stick to your own way of doing things.

## 2 WEDNESDAY

*Moon Age Day 18 Moon Sign Aries*

You could be all fingers and thumbs today, which is exactly why you should leave any delicate jobs at least until tomorrow. There are some crucial decisions to be made soon, if not by you, then by someone in the vicinity. If someone asks your opinion, be prepared to tell the truth.

## 3 THURSDAY

*Moon Age Day 19 Moon Sign Taurus*

A deep understanding of specific situations lies at the heart of your efforts today. Don't allow yourself to be bullied into doing anything that goes against the grain and allow your conscience to rule your decision-making. A good day for romance and for allowing personal matters to take their course.

## 4 FRIDAY

*Moon Age Day 20 Moon Sign Taurus*

Nostalgia might be tugging at your heartstrings on one or two occasions today. Maybe you are looking at some old family snaps or meeting someone you haven't seen for quite some time. Whatever the reason, you also need to be aware that life is for living now, rather than dwelling on the past.

## 5 SATURDAY

*Moon Age Day 21 Moon Sign Gemini*

Romantic issues suit you well today and act as a sort of platform for your ego, which is strong at this time. A busy day is in store, so it would be sensible to be out of bed and active early. Confidence is not hard to find, but shows more when you are doing things you really understand.

## 6 SUNDAY

*Moon Age Day 22 Moon Sign Gemini*

There are many things you want to get done today, but whether you get around to tackling them remains to be seen. What would really suit you best might be a change of scene and the chance to look at rolling oceans or high hills. If you are able to be in the company of people you really love, so much the better.

## 7 MONDAY *Moon Age Day 23 Moon Sign Cancer*

Progress is not fast today in work matters, but is more noticeable in terms of relationships. If you are lucky, there could be good news where your finances are concerned. Leave some of the more boring jobs for others to do, especially family members who may not be pulling their weight.

## 8 TUESDAY *Moon Age Day 24 Moon Sign Cancer*

You can be somewhat touchy today and your ego can quite easily be deflated. At the same time, you show a great sense of humour, which could be of great importance when you are dealing with people who seem to be simply born awkward. A small family dilemma may end up being another cause for hilarity.

## 9 WEDNESDAY *Moon Age Day 25 Moon Sign Cancer*

Your powers of persuasion are quite strong now, leading you into situations that mean getting your own way far more than you might have expected. Even where you do find yourself up against it, the natural good nature displayed by Virgo at its best is easy to see. With the weekend a few days away, you will want to do some planning now.

## 10 THURSDAY *Moon Age Day 26 Moon Sign Leo*

A few sharp comments made by you today might not go down all that well with certain other people. You need to be very careful what you say, because there are some sensitive types around and you can be quite prickly. Stay around people you know well, because they are less likely to react to your mood.

## 11 FRIDAY *Moon Age Day 27 Moon Sign Leo*

Now you find a way to improve your present financial status, no matter how much you have to chance your arm to do so. Because you are feeling extremely confident in your own abilities and your forward planning skills, you can afford to take the sort of calculated risk that you might normally leave well alone.

## 12 SATURDAY *Moon Age Day 28 Moon Sign Virgo*

**There isn't much doubt that you find yourself in the best position of all to make significant progress. The level of courage you display is high right now and you don't mind confronting issues if necessary. Support for your plans is good, mainly because of your own attitude.**

## 13 SUNDAY *Moon Age Day 0 Moon Sign Virgo*

**You have a part to play in major decisions in the middle of the month. Today should reflect a host of positive trends, both professional and social. With a new week ahead you could decide to make Sunday evening very special and this is one of those times when you can afford to burn the candle at both ends.**

## 14 MONDAY *Moon Age Day 1 Moon Sign Virgo*

**Look out for a day of contrasts. Family issues should be going well, but you might not be able to get all your own way as far as personal matters are concerned. Meanwhile, the pressures that are being put on you at work could begin to show, with the result that you tell people exactly how you feel.**

## 15 TUESDAY *Moon Age Day 2 Moon Sign Libra*

You certainly have the ability to command attention today and should be turning heads wherever you go. Now definitely pulling away from restrictions, you are more progressive and should feel generally better in yourself. This is not lost on those around you, who recognise your cheerful ways.

## 16 WEDNESDAY *Moon Age Day 3 Moon Sign Libra*

You could easily find yourself in a prominent position today, so you will need to keep your wits about you. Being in the limelight is a two-edged sword for Virgo; you often like it, but sometimes hate it. Fortunately, you are not feeling particularly shy at present.

## 17 THURSDAY *Moon Age Day 4 Moon Sign Scorpio*

You should now be feeling buoyed up physically and ready to face whatever challenges come your way. If for any reason you have been lacking in stamina in recent days, the situation is now reversed. Challenges are something you will relish and the busier you are, the better you are likely to feel.

## 18 FRIDAY  *Moon Age Day 5 Moon Sign Scorpio*

Your mind is sharp and your sense of humour definitely intact. This gives you the ability to get ahead of the game and to show the world at large what you are made of. The weekend ahead is comprised in part of positive social encounters, most of which are geared towards improving your personal situation.

## 19 SATURDAY ☿ *Moon Age Day 6 Moon Sign Scorpio*

The pace of everyday life is clearly quite rapid at present, so much so that you don't really have time to stop and take a breath. Be specific in your conversations with others because if there is something you want, you need to ask for it plainly. Most people will respect your present honesty and integrity.

## 20 SUNDAY ☿ *Moon Age Day 7 Moon Sign Sagittarius*

A happy focus on domestic issues and home life in general should make for a reasonably comfortable sort of Sunday. Your ideas are not quite as grandiose as they have been across the last few days, but you show yourself as being gentle and caring. A couple of calculated gambles could pay off.

## 21 MONDAY ☿ *Moon Age Day 8 Moon Sign Sagittarius*

This is a good period for broadening your mind and for coming to new and quite revolutionary conclusions, sometimes about yourself. Keep an open mind with regard to the activities of certain friends, but don't be badgered into actions that genuinely go against the grain as far as you are concerned.

## 22 TUESDAY ☿ *Moon Age Day 9 Moon Sign Capricorn*

Issues of personality might put you on the spot today, meaning that you cannot hide in the shadows regarding any issue you feel particularly strongly about. Don't be reticent in speaking your mind just because you know others won't agree with your point of view. If you explain yourself, you can win out in the end.

## 23 WEDNESDAY ☿ *Moon Age Day 10 Moon Sign Capricorn*

You will probably have your work cut out today if you try to show people how much you care about them. In the end you might simply have to tell them one last time and leave it at that, because you can't cater for everyone's paranoia. Life is busy right now and financial prospects look well starred.

## 24 THURSDAY ☿ *Moon Age Day 11 Moon Sign Aquarius*

The Sun has now moved into your solar second house, where it is going to be much more use to you in material terms. It helps you to build on recent successes, but the personality cult that has started to build around you is somewhat diminished. You also begin to work better in team situations.

## 25 FRIDAY ☿ *Moon Age Day 12 Moon Sign Aquarius*

Emotional matters can put you in the hot seat, though probably not if you explain yourself right from the start. As long as you are being genuinely honest, all is well. What won't work right now is pulling the wool over someone's eyes, even though you are simply trying to avoid hurting them.

## 26 SATURDAY ☿ *Moon Age Day 13 Moon Sign Pisces*

The lunar low makes it much easier for you to watch life happen, rather than specifically taking part all that much. Nevertheless there is work to be done, and even if you don't feel like starting it you will be better off later. Stay away from people who seem determined to drop you in it or who won't co-operate.

## 27 SUNDAY ☿ *Moon Age Day 14 Moon Sign Pisces*

There are slight setbacks to everyday progress, but it would be fair to say that the lunar low does not have the same part to play in your day as appeared to be the case yesterday. Maybe it is because you are keeping busy and probably getting out of the house at some stage. A little shopping might not go amiss.

## 28 MONDAY ☿ *Moon Age Day 15 Moon Sign Aries*

There is the potential for good fortune to come your way and you should be handling cash well. Looking ahead isn't difficult, leading to a shrewd but speculative frame of mind. There should be plenty of compliments coming your way, which might make you confused about how others think about you.

## 29 TUESDAY ☿ *Moon Age Day 16 Moon Sign Aries*

Lively discussions seem to be the order of the day as September draws towards its close. Keep your comments on any situation brief but honest and you won't go far wrong. Feelings of excitement might be somewhat justified by the promise of even better times to come, so you can afford to be optimistic.

## 30 WEDNESDAY ☿ *Moon Age Day 17 Moon Sign Taurus*

This is a time of steady but relentless building, both in a financial and a personal sense. As a result, you should be quite happy because the most positive associations of Virgo are given endless scope. Try not to be too fussy about details and stick to what you know when it comes to public discussions.

## Your Month at a Glance

⊕ = Opportunities are around ⊖ = Be on the defensive ○ = Life is pretty ordinary

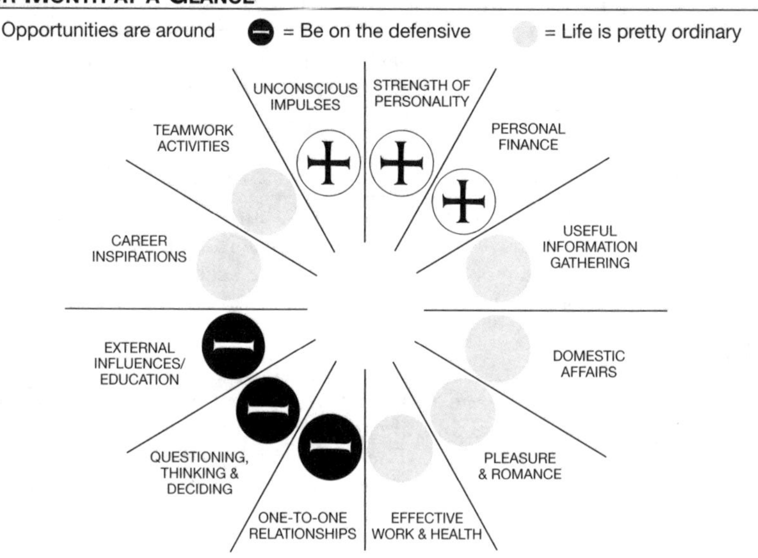


## October Highs and Lows

*Here I show you how the rhythms of the Moon will affect you this month. Like the tide, your energies and abilities will rise and fall with its pattern. When it is above the centre line, go for it, when it is below, you should be resting.*

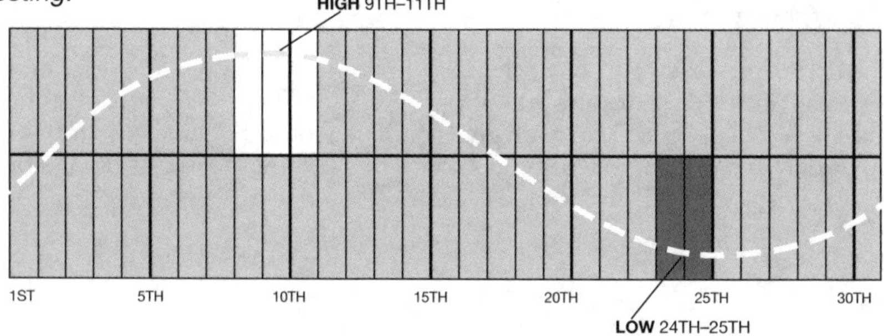

## 1 THURSDAY ☿ *Moon Age Day 18 Moon Sign Taurus*

There are some wonderful surprises in store for Virgo today, but you will have to keep your eye on the ball to gain from any of them. Not everyone is on your side at work, but those who aren't probably have something to gain from opposing you. Focus on your own circumstances and don't rise to the bait!

## 2 FRIDAY ☿ *Moon Age Day 19 Moon Sign Gemini*

A time of social highlights comes along, with plenty of opportunities to have fun. Present astrological trends could lead you to cast your mind forward to the medium-term future, perhaps even Christmas. Longer term plans might have to be put on hold for a variety of different and generally tedious reasons.

## 3 SATURDAY ☿ *Moon Age Day 20 Moon Sign Gemini*

You definitely enjoy being busy today and can make the best out of almost any sort of situation. Watch out for the odd minor mishap, probably brought about as a result of carelessness exhibited by someone else. Your present quick thinking makes you good to have around in any tight corner.

## 4 SUNDAY ☿ *Moon Age Day 21 Moon Sign Gemini*

Romance not only becomes more likely, but potentially more rewarding, too. Things that irritated you earlier in the week are now much more likely to make you laugh instead. It might be good to look for a change of scene and an alteration in your routines this Sunday. Money matters may also begin to look stronger.

## 5 MONDAY ☿ *Moon Age Day 22 Moon Sign Cancer*

Now is the time to be enjoying good social trends and letting people know just how capable you are. Controlling all aspects of your life isn't going to be particularly easy, but you care less about certain issues at this time. Relationships should be working out particularly well and offering new insights.

## 6 TUESDAY ☿ *Moon Age Day 23 Moon Sign Cancer*

There are warnings of a rather more problematic series of trends for today, some of which could find you disagreeing with people who normally are no problem. The fault could be yours, so it is important to stand back and look again. As long as you are reasonable, any sort of compromise eventually becomes possible.

## 7 WEDNESDAY ☿ *Moon Age Day 24 Moon Sign Leo*

Professional developments should be working out quite well, leaving you with more time to please yourself. If life is plain sailing, take some time out. The year is growing older and there are still some personal incentives you have not looked at specifically. A big plan is worth another, very careful look now.

## 8 THURSDAY ☿ *Moon Age Day 25 Moon Sign Leo*

It is likely you could talk anyone into doing anything for you now. There are one or two individuals around at present whom you look at with slight mistrust, though probably for no good reason. There won't be time to do everything you would wish today, so it is important to look carefully at priorities.

## 9 FRIDAY ☿ *Moon Age Day 26 Moon Sign Virgo*

**The Moon moves gradually into your zodiac sign today, and brings with it a desire to do as much as you can, as quickly as proves to be possible. Despite a wealth of opportunities it would advisable to tackle jobs one at a time. At least that way you can be sure you do all of them to the best of your ability.**

## 10 SATURDAY  *Moon Age Day 27 Moon Sign Virgo*

**The Moon is still on your side, so get cracking and keep busy. With everything to prove and a vitality that is second to none, it's unlikely that you will be overlooked in anything. Routines are really for the birds at this time and you tend to do whatever takes your fancy, at the time that seems most providential.**

## 11 SUNDAY  *Moon Age Day 28 Moon Sign Virgo*

**Talks with others can find you making a sort of headway you hadn't been expecting. For many of you, this is a day of rest, but you've been there and done that earlier this week. As a result, don't be surprised to find yourself out of bed early and anxious to get on with life just as quickly as you are able.**

## 12 MONDAY *Moon Age Day 29 Moon Sign Libra*

There are signs that this could prove to be one of the better days of the month for your romantic life. There are overtures likely to come from both expected and unexpected directions and a wealth of interest from friends, too. If everyone seems to be talking about you, that's because you are so interesting now.

## 13 TUESDAY
*Moon Age Day 0 Moon Sign Libra*

Much of the day is geared towards practical matters, though it doesn't have to be that way. Virtually nothing in your life would fall apart if you decided to take some time off. There are people around who long for your company and a host of activities that are going the way you would wish. Enjoy yourself for a while.

## 14 WEDNESDAY
*Moon Age Day 1 Moon Sign Scorpio*

Right now, making up your mind regarding even a crucial personal matter is not going to be at all easy. It might be best to defer decisions until later. By that time you will have had the chance to seek out the advice of someone you trust implicitly. Friends are easy to make at this time, and are not likely to be lost later.

## 15 THURSDAY
*Moon Age Day 2 Moon Sign Scorpio*

The practical world is still doing you the odd favour, allowing you to make gains, particularly in a financial sense. Rules and regulations are not too difficult to follow now and you find yourself well able to conform when it is necessary. Help a friend with a specific problem and also be supportive of family members.

## 16 FRIDAY
*Moon Age Day 3 Moon Sign Scorpio*

This is a time during which love life and relationships should be putting a very definite smile on your face. If you don't have the time to do everything you wish in a practical sense, be willing to leave some of it for another day. Most of the people you meet today prove to be very reasonable.

## 17 SATURDAY
*Moon Age Day 4 Moon Sign Sagittarius*

You are at your very best now in small gatherings, and especially so when mixing with people you already know. The slightly shy side of Virgo is showing and you also demonstrate a reserve that casual acquaintances might not understand. Nevertheless, in a professional sense, you still display confidence.

## 18 SUNDAY
*Moon Age Day 5 Moon Sign Sagittarius*

You may discover that some people are far less assertive than usual, and you can put that down to your own attitude. It is a fact that you don't brook any interference right now and that those around you realise the fact. The more you get done early today, the greater is the likelihood that you can enjoy a peaceful Sunday later.

## 19 MONDAY *Moon Age Day 6 Moon Sign Capricorn*

Only you can decide whether to believe everything you hear today, but there could be some fibbers around. Mostly, these will represent people who are charming and quite incapable of doing you any harm, but you need to be on your guard all the same. Keep an eye on your health.

## 20 TUESDAY *Moon Age Day 7 Moon Sign Capricorn*

Today could be a mixed bag, but is still likely to favour you in a general sense. If there are any frustrations, these are likely to come about as a result of the attitude of colleagues, some of whom are ploughing a very different furrow from your own. Keep abreast of things that are happening in your immediate locality.

## 21 WEDNESDAY *Moon Age Day 8 Moon Sign Capricorn*

Work and practical affairs keep you generally busy today and offer you the comfort of knowing that life is running in a smooth and steady way. There probably won't be too much in the way of excitement, though you are hardly likely to be worried by that fact at the moment.

## 22 THURSDAY *Moon Age Day 9 Moon Sign Aquarius*

You may discover that in financial matters you have to take a very patient point of view, which could make it difficult to be immediate in your approach. This can lead to some inner conflict because you really do want to get ahead today. Creative potential remains essentially high, with some wonderful ideas coming along.

## 23 FRIDAY *Moon Age Day 10 Moon Sign Aquarius*

Although you are feeling quite assertive today, you do need to watch your step in some ways. Not everyone is working towards your ultimate good, no matter what they say to the contrary. Problems are not likely to arise with relatives or friends, though colleagues could be more of a problem.

## 24 SATURDAY *Moon Age Day 11 Moon Sign Pisces*

A two-day lunar low is at hand. Normally this might be a cause for some concern, but you have been pushing yourself so hard of late, a reduction in pressure ought to be no bad thing. Comfort and security are on your mind now and you might even decide to take a day more or less completely to yourself.

## 25 SUNDAY *Moon Age Day 12 Moon Sign Pisces*

When things get quiet, Virgo subjects can spend time pampering themselves. Why not? You have put in a great deal of effort so far this month and you deserve to have a decent rest. On the other hand, if you have to work today do as little as you can and allow others to fill in where possible. This could be a fairly uneventful day.

## 26 MONDAY *Moon Age Day 13 Moon Sign Aries*

Today should be reasonably fulfilling in a workaday sense, though better still in terms of your social and personal life. Romance seems to rear its head on a number of occasions, and particularly so if you put yourself out. This might be a good time to buy someone a bunch of flowers or some other small gift.

## 27 TUESDAY *Moon Age Day 14 Moon Sign Aries*

You need to get on with something simple and relatively free from stress if it proves to be at all possible right now. You don't have too much energy in reserve, which is why you are willing to let others do things that you would normally wish to deal with yourself. When they do, avoid being critical of their methods.

## 28 WEDNESDAY *Moon Age Day 15 Moon Sign Taurus*

Right now you have the knack of getting your point of view across in a very positive way and can really get on famously when in the company of people whose attitude stimulates you in any way. Frank, free and quite outspoken, you can definitely make today your own with only a little effort.

## 29 THURSDAY *Moon Age Day 16 Moon Sign Taurus*

Present relationships tend to be quite harmonious, even with people you don't always trust too much. Those folk you have seen as competitors now want to help you out, that is, if you are not too suspicious to take their help on board. You seem to be quite intuitive at present and can easily make up your mind about anything.

## 30 FRIDAY *Moon Age Day 17 Moon Sign Gemini*

Your acquisitive tendencies are strong now, which isn't so strange for the zodiac sign of Virgo. You know what you want from life, and have a pretty good idea about how you intend to get it. Some would call you calculating, but since you bear the good of others in mind, this isn't really the case.

## 31 SATURDAY *Moon Age Day 18 Moon Sign Gemini*

Good times in relationships mark the weekend out as feeling safe, warm and generally comfortable. Although you can't count on the support of everyone you know, in the main the people you rely on the most come up trumps on your behalf. Concentrate on issues that can make you better off financially.

# November

2015

## Your Month at a Glance

(+) = Opportunities are around (−) = Be on the defensive ( ) = Life is pretty ordinary

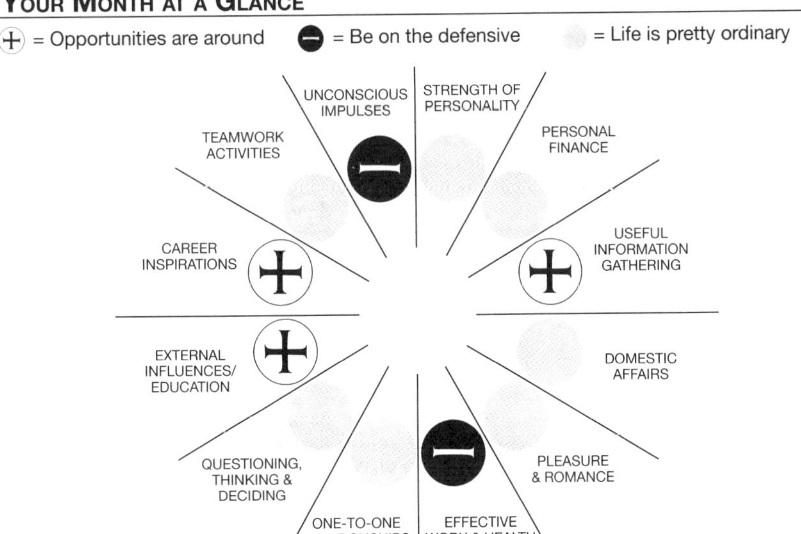


## November Highs and Lows

*Here I show you how the rhythms of the Moon will affect you this month. Like the tide, your energies and abilities will rise and fall with its pattern. When it is above the centre line, go for it, when it is below, you should be resting.*

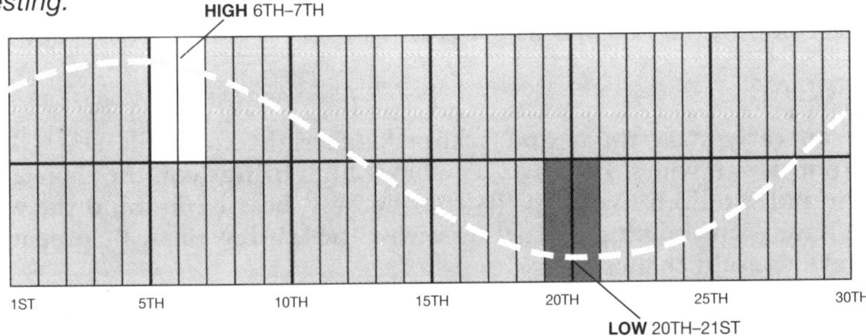

## 1 SUNDAY
*Moon Age Day 19 Moon Sign Cancer*

The pursuit of wealth might now be on your list of priorities. Virgo may not be the most acquisitive of the zodiac signs, but it isn't too far behind. It's all down to a sense of security, which Virgo desires. Casting your mind forward in time, you can now do some deals that will feather your nest in years to come.

## 2 MONDAY
*Moon Age Day 20 Moon Sign Cancer*

Stay clear of disagreements today if you possibly can. It would be better not to interact too much with people at all, rather than to find yourself involved in pointless rows. Such a state of affairs is far less likely in terms of deep attachments. Virgo subjects who are looking for love should have some success now.

## 3 TUESDAY
*Moon Age Day 21 Moon Sign Leo*

The period during which help is at hand if you need it continues apace, so don't assume you have do everything for yourself now. On the contrary, people are only too willing to put themselves out on your behalf and will continue to do so for a while. Even those you don't know very well can be considerate.

## 4 WEDNESDAY
*Moon Age Day 22 Moon Sign Leo*

The most powerful focus today is upon close, personal attachments, but that doesn't mean you are ignoring the world at large. On the contrary, you virtually demand to be out there in the middle of whatever is happening. You might not see all that much of family members today because you are likely to be so busy.

## 5 THURSDAY
*Moon Age Day 23 Moon Sign Leo*

There isn't a great deal of dynamic ambition today, but this is only a very short trend and due to end almost immediately. For the moment, you will be happy to watch life go by and less inclined than of late to look for riotous social company. Part of your nature is actually very nostalgic around now.

## 6 FRIDAY
*Moon Age Day 24 Moon Sign Virgo*

**Get an early start today and acknowledge right from the start that fortune now favours the brave. The lunar high brings you the chance to shine and should lift your spirits considerably, bearing in mind the way you have been thinking and acting across the last few days. Be prepared to take the odd chance.**

## 7 SATURDAY *Moon Age Day 25 Moon Sign Virgo*

**Another potentially good day and a time during which you will be making the most of just about any opportunity that comes your way. Creatively speaking you know what looks and feels right and you can gain support from some unexpected directions. You could surprise yourself with your boldness right now.**

## 8 SUNDAY *Moon Age Day 26 Moon Sign Libra*

A change of scene would suit you down to the ground, even though the necessities of life could make that somewhat difficult to achieve. You should remain fairly busy and be concentrating on making things better for yourself in a financial sense especially. Family demands are present, though easy to deal with.

## 9 MONDAY *Moon Age Day 27 Moon Sign Libra*

When tasks have to be completed today, you are inclined to want to do everything your own way. That's fine, just as long as you can persuade others that you know what you are talking about. There will be some awkward types around at the moment, so you could have to work quite hard to get the message across.

## 10 TUESDAY *Moon Age Day 28 Moon Sign Libra*

You might feel that you are less in control of your own life in some ways, but this should not really prove to be a particular issue as long as you are willing to co-operate with others. Get on side with those who have ideas that broadly parallel your own and don't be afraid to take a few calculated risks.

## 11 WEDNESDAY *Moon Age Day 29 Moon Sign Scorpio*

Someone might be trying to put you down in the estimation of others, or at least that's how it will appear to you right now. It is likely that you are not looking at things quite as logically as would normally be the case and emotions can get in the way. Most important is to keep a smile on your face, even when you feel jumpy.

## 12 THURSDAY *Moon Age Day 0 Moon Sign Scorpio*

This is not a day during which you can afford to take anything for granted. You should check and double-check all details, especially if any of them are related to travel. Staying in one place could prove to be something of a bind, particularly when movement looks so potentially interesting and rewarding.

## 13 FRIDAY *Moon Age Day 1 Moon Sign Sagittarius*

Your love life is apt to be a high point today. Single Virgo subjects ought to find a good deal of attention coming their way, whilst those involved in settled relationships can achieve an even better understanding and contentment. Practical progress could be slightly restricted, but since you are busy in other ways, it won't matter.

## 14 SATURDAY *Moon Age Day 2 Moon Sign Sagittarius*

You can probably expect a good deal more attention coming your way around this time. This will happen in both a personal and in a more general sense. Popularity is everything to you now and you won't hold back in terms of the love you offer in return. Almost anyone can feel your warmth now.

## 15 SUNDAY *Moon Age Day 3 Moon Sign Sagittarius*

A more settled period comes along as far as your personal life is concerned. Don't be too quick to offer advice, because you could find yourself refusing the same suggestions yourself before very long. Courage is necessary in public situations but you should come good in sporting activities.

## 16 MONDAY *Moon Age Day 4 Moon Sign Capricorn*

Minor disruptions to domestic peace and harmony typify the sort of trends that stand around you right now. Try not to get more involved in them than is strictly necessary and definitely stay away from other people's rows. You need peace and quiet, though whether you can find it today remains to be seen.

## 17 TUESDAY *Moon Age Day 5 Moon Sign Capricorn*

It's a time for getting down to the real nitty-gritty of issues. Don't be sidetracked and make certain that you know others are telling the truth. How can you be certain? Well, at the moment your intuition is turned up high, so few people will be able to fool you.

## 18 WEDNESDAY *Moon Age Day 6 Moon Sign Aquarius*

Things could be slightly sluggish in a professional sense, so it would be best to only do what you have to at work. Domestically speaking, life should be rather easier to address and in truth, you will be happiest today when at home. You might relish the prospect of simply putting your feet up.

## 19 THURSDAY *Moon Age Day 7 Moon Sign Aquarius*

Friends could turn out to be quite helpful, often in fairly unexpected ways. Don't be too proud to accept assistance if it's offered, even though in at least some cases you could manage better on your own. Keep a sense of proportion when dealing with issues that have stumped you in the past. Persistence pays off in the end.

## 20 FRIDAY *Moon Age Day 8 Moon Sign Pisces*

You could find yourself receiving support, rather than offering it. Potentially speaking, the arrival of the lunar low can take the wind out of your sails, but if you are prepared, the situation will not be half so bad. There are confidences to keep, and although practical matters are on the back burner, love and attention are very noticeable.

## 21 SATURDAY *Moon Age Day 9 Moon Sign Pisces*

Compromise is your middle name today, or at least it if isn't, then it should be. You can get more today by being willing to give a little than at just about any other time this month. Some nostalgia creeps in, but that is part of the way the lunar low makes its presence felt in your life. By tomorrow you will be flying high again.

## 22 SUNDAY *Moon Age Day 10 Moon Sign Aries*

You will have to fall back on your own wits today, because people are not all that reliable. The problem is that you have very exacting standards at present and won't be too keen to relinquish control in any case. Be prepared to alter your ideas when circumstances don't turn out as you may have expected.

## 23 MONDAY *Moon Age Day 11 Moon Sign Aries*

You should feel good about yourself and life in general as the week gets started. There is tremendous scope for advancement at work, plus extra incentive to go out and get what you want. Although you will come across obstacles at some stage during the day, these are unlikely to hold you back.

## 24 TUESDAY *Moon Age Day 12 Moon Sign Taurus*

A generally lucrative period continues, though you won't have everything you would wish today. Part of the reason for this is that some of your expectations are not entirely realistic. This will lead to disappointments if you fail to realise how life really is. A more contemplative phase is needed.

## 25 WEDNESDAY *Moon Age Day 13 Moon Sign Taurus*

Your mind works swiftly, leading you to arrive at some quite staggering conclusions and often on the spur of the moment. The middle of the working week makes specific demands of you, and especially so at work. You may be quite pleased to lay down some responsibilities by the evening.

## 26 THURSDAY *Moon Age Day 14 Moon Sign Gemini*

There is little time for intimate concerns today, because material and practical considerations are taking up so much of your time. All things considered, this would be an ideal time to take a day off, though the way your mind is working at the moment this is less than likely.

## 27 FRIDAY *Moon Age Day 15 Moon Sign Gemini*

Work-wise, someone may be putting you in the picture regarding an issue that has been at the forefront of your mind of late. Getting to know what is going on in your vicinity seems especially important now, which is why you are listening so carefully to everything that is being said.

## 28 SATURDAY *Moon Age Day 16 Moon Sign Cancer*

A thoughtful approach to specific matters is necessary early in the day, but by the afternoon you should be feeling quite active again. You respond very well to the overtures of your partner and will be quite happy to get out of the house. Perhaps a shopping trip is on the cards.

## 29 SUNDAY *Moon Age Day 17 Moon Sign Cancer*

You have little real patience with specific emotional matters today and you may consider that someone you know well is acting in a fairly irrational manner. There are some unusual people about whose ideas and actions could fascinate you somewhat, but don't be drawn into anything weird.

## 30 MONDAY *Moon Age Day 18 Moon Sign Cancer*

Personal concerns or wishes can be successfully addressed today, perhaps partly as a result of information that comes through the post or over the internet. Concern for your friends is also apparent, as you try to help someone sort out a thorny problem associated with relationships.

# December 2015

## Your Month at a Glance

(+) = Opportunities are around (−) = Be on the defensive ( ) = Life is pretty ordinary

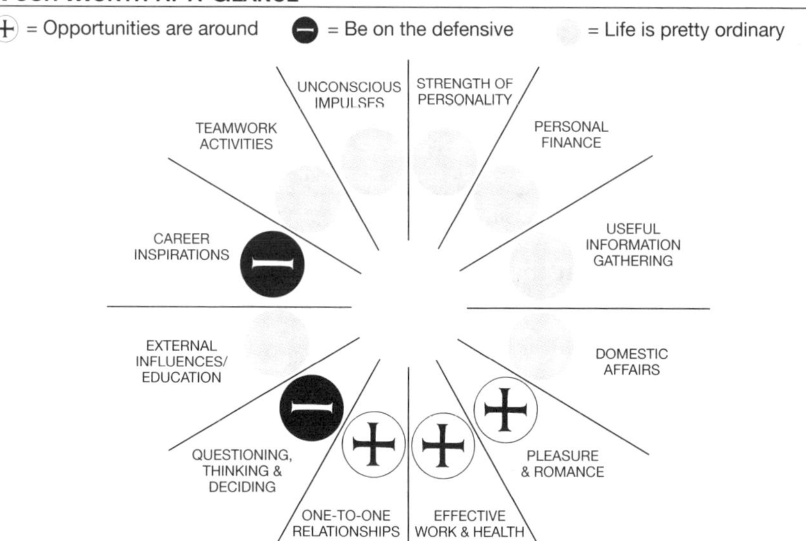


## December Highs and Lows

*Here I show you how the rhythms of the Moon will affect you this month. Like the tide, your energies and abilities will rise and fall with its pattern. When it is above the centre line, go for it, when it is below, you should be resting.*

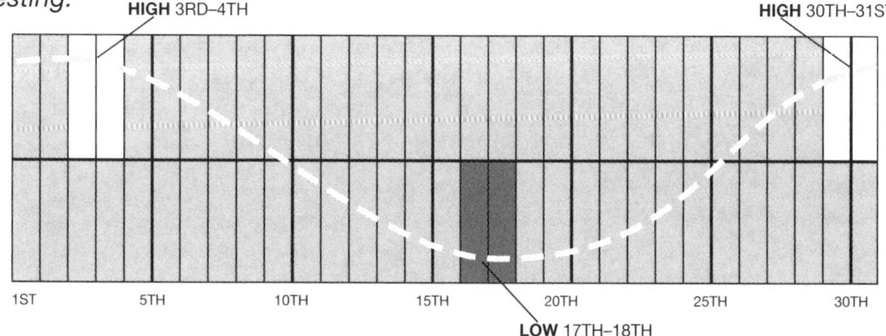

## 1 TUESDAY *Moon Age Day 19 Moon Sign Leo*

You are well aware what elements of your life deserve your attention today, even though one or two people might think that they know different. Spend time with family members and do what you can to support a friend who could well be going through a rough period right now.

## 2 WEDNESDAY *Moon Age Day 20 Moon Sign Leo*

Compromises in relationships are a natural part of what you will encounter at the present time. If you refuse to make them, problems could come along later. Stay away from rows in your family or indeed amongst friends. The problem is not one of failing to hold your own, but rather of being too aggressive.

## 3 THURSDAY *Moon Age Day 21 Moon Sign Virgo*

**The start of the months sees you reaching your mental and physical peak. It doesn't matter what you take on today, you have the energy and determination to see it through properly. Gains can be made as a result of meetings and discussions that could have taken place some time ago.**

## 4 FRIDAY *Moon Age Day 22 Moon Sign Virgo*

**This is still very much a go-ahead period and offers you the vitality to get everything you need to be done out of the way before the weekend. You ought to be in fine spirits and more than willing to have a go at more or less anything. Stay away from contentious topics in conversation.**

## 5 SATURDAY *Moon Age Day 23 Moon Sign Libra*

Some of your efforts at keeping life under control are going wrong. The results are likely to be more amusing than annoying, though there could be times today when the odd frustration will creep in. Once again, it is important to avoid confrontation with people who are not really worth your effort.

## 6 SUNDAY *Moon Age Day 24 Moon Sign Libra*

Although there is little in the way of harmony in your relationships today, part of the reason could be frustrations you find difficult to address. Talk to people and truly listen to what they have to say. Compromise is necessary and that isn't a particularly tall order for you at the moment.

## 7 MONDAY *Moon Age Day 25 Moon Sign Libra*

Though career aims might have rather less going for them than has been the case lately, you should certainly be enjoying yourself in terms of your personal life. Compliments are easy to come by and you are likely to turn heads wherever you go, especially by the evening.

## 8 TUESDAY *Moon Age Day 26 Moon Sign Scorpio*

Financially speaking, there could be some minor improvements now – and not a moment too soon, with Christmas so close. Nevertheless, you need to spend wisely and to look out for those bargains that lie around every corner. All in all, this could be one of the best days of December for shopping.

## 9 WEDNESDAY *Moon Age Day 27 Moon Sign Scorpio*

Personal and intimate matters are the most rewarding of all this Wednesday. You will be quite busy moment by moment, but you need to save time to show your lover how much you care. The response you get is very positive and should see you finishing the day on a high note.

## 10 THURSDAY *Moon Age Day 28 Moon Sign Sagittarius*

You could easily get the feeling that you are speaking out of turn today. That's fine, but unless you say what you think, how on earth will others know? It's really a case of speaking the truth to shame the devil, just as long as you remember to use a little Mercurial tact on the way.

## 11 FRIDAY *Moon Age Day 0 Moon Sign Sagittarius*

The time is right to establish good relations with just about anyone, even people who have not been your favourites in the past. There is a good chance that you are being taken more seriously now and that you might make a friend of someone who was never very kind to you in years gone by.

## 12 SATURDAY *Moon Age Day 1 Moon Sign Sagittarius*

Although today starts out fairly steady, things could soon hot up. Progress is hard to see at first, which is why by lunchtime you'll have to put in that extra bit of effort that can make all the difference. By the evening, you can be the life and soul of any party. If there isn't one on offer, you might create a shindig yourself.

## 13 SUNDAY *Moon Age Day 2 Moon Sign Capricorn*

You might have a sense today that you can't rely on anyone except yourself. Up to a point that might be the case, but you ought to give friends the benefit of the doubt all the same. Offer others a helping hand in specific tasks that are familiar to you, but don't get in the way if younger people are seeking independence.

## 14 MONDAY *Moon Age Day 3 Moon Sign Capricorn*

You could be in quite a hurry to complete a particular project and will be quite anxious not to allow anything to get in your way. In all probability this is something you should have done days or weeks ago, but right now is hardly the right time to address it. Put it on the shelf until the New Year.

## 15 TUESDAY *Moon Age Day 4 Moon Sign Aquarius*

Beware a heavy-handed approach at home, particularly with younger people, who are only seeking to spread their wings. You should learn to trust, as others are willing to trust you. Only rarely are you likely to be let down. Confidence to do the right thing is there, but you need to look for it.

## 16 WEDNESDAY *Moon Age Day 5 Moon Sign Aquarius*

Your social instincts are very definitely engaged today and you can be the best company imaginable. This is far from being a normal sort of Wednesday as far as you are concerned, even if you have to work. When you are not toiling, there are gains to be made through love and new friendship.

## 17 THURSDAY *Moon Age Day 6 Moon Sign Pisces*

Get ready for a couple of days during which it will be difficult to get everything you want from life. The lunar low is holding you back, but not all that much. As long as you stick to planning, and leave a few of the more concrete jobs until the very end of the week, you will hardly be held up at all this month.

## 18 FRIDAY *Moon Age Day 7 Moon Sign Pisces*

Stick to the simple things of life and spend some time spoiling yourself. There is an active and very demanding period ahead, so it won't do you any harm to charge up those batteries. Confidence isn't really dented, unless you come face to face with people who seem determined to put you down.

## 19 SATURDAY *Moon Age Day 8 Moon Sign Aries*

Get ready to make tracks and get ahead professionally. With one eye on Christmas and the other on what you want to achieve materially, there isn't a great deal of time to spare right now. Don't overbook yourself for the weekend. It's the last one before Christmas and there might be shopping you have forgotten.

## 20 SUNDAY *Moon Age Day 9 Moon Sign Aries*

Getting along with others isn't too difficult this weekend, just as long as they are willing to do exactly what you ask. There is a danger that you are being rather more selfish than usual. Get out and about, if you can, though it is likely that your main destination will be the local shopping centre.

## 21 MONDAY *Moon Age Day 10 Moon Sign Aries*

Communication issues are to the fore today and you need to make sure that you get any message across intact. Don't be too quick to judge others for merely doing things you have done yourself in the past. It would be sensible to take a sympathetic point of view when possible today.

## 22 TUESDAY *Moon Age Day 11 Moon Sign Taurus*

Yet again, the circumstances surrounding your home life and domestic issues generally seem to be going your way. There is a great sense of comfort and security about now, mixed with a tinge of nostalgia, probably on account of the time of year. Despite this, you must be realistic.

## 23 WEDNESDAY *Moon Age Day 12 Moon Sign Taurus*

You now seem to be in such a hurry to get things done, you are forgetting some of the most important details. If you want to avoid having to stop and then begin all over again, you need to concentrate. Friends are there to lend a helping hand, if you give them the chance.

## 24 THURSDAY *Moon Age Day 13 Moon Sign Gemini*

There are almost certainly some surprises on the social scene, together with a desire to get on well with people generally. Because you are a Virgo, it is likely that you have everything prepared. Don't be at all surprised if nostalgic associations take over at some stage during the day, particularly if you have children.

## 25 FRIDAY *Moon Age Day 14 Moon Sign Gemini*

A lovely mix of planetary trends surrounds you during Christmas Day. Some of them are quiet, so you may not choose to be socially active all the time. You receive significant emotional support and return it in kind. Not surprisingly, family associations are well accented right now.

## 26 SATURDAY *Moon Age Day 15 Moon Sign Cancer*

It is the home-based side of Christmas that appeals to you the most this time around, though you are chatty, carefree and very good company in any situation. There could be presents of a very singular nature coming your way, one or two of them from a most unexpected direction.

## 27 SUNDAY *Moon Age Day 16 Moon Sign Cancer*

Love affairs are well highlighted today, as is travel. Perhaps you will see people you haven't shared an hour or two with for quite a long time. Although you might be bullied into doing things that go against the grain, you could be quite surprised in the end. It is worth putting yourself out.

## 28 MONDAY *Moon Age Day 17 Moon Sign Leo*

Whatever you decide to take on board today, bear in mind that energies are limited and that your recovery rate is not what it might normally be. Because of this, you need to restrict your activities just a little, whilst at the same time making yourself fully conversant with what is happening around you.

## 29 TUESDAY *Moon Age Day 18 Moon Sign Leo*

Don't be surprised if the general pace of events tends to slow significantly around this time. There are quieter astrological trends predominating today, not the least of which is supplied by the Moon. Being where it is at present, it turns your attention specifically in the direction of home and family.

## 30 WEDNESDAY *Moon Age Day 19 Moon Sign Virgo*

**You may be in for the best and most protracted New Year bash you have known for years. Today and tomorrow coincide with the lunar high, offering a fun-filled attitude, together with an instinctive knowledge regarding how to keep other people laughing. Almost anything you do today is tinged with genius.**

## 31 THURSDAY *Moon Age Day 20 Moon Sign Virgo*

**It appears that this is a particularly good phase for any sort of intimacy between yourself and your partner. For those who are not attached, it might be that a friendship takes on a different sort of meaning in your life. Resolutions made today are likely to be as a result of a great deal of thought earlier in the year.**

# How to Calculate Your Rising Sign

Most astrologers agree that, next to the Sun Sign, the most important influence on any person is the Rising Sign at the time of their birth. The Rising Sign represents the astrological sign that was rising over the eastern horizon when each and every one of us came into the world. It is sometimes also called the Ascendant.

Let us suppose, for example, that you were born with the Sun in the zodiac sign of Libra. This would bestow certain characteristics on you that are likely to be shared by all other Librans. However, a Libran with Aries Rising would show a very different attitude towards life, and of course relationships, than a Libran with Pisces Rising.

For these reasons, this book shows how your zodiac Rising Sign has a bearing on all the possible positions of the Sun at birth. Simply look through the Aries table opposite.

As long as you know your approximate time of birth the graph will show you how to discover your Rising Sign.

Look across the top of the graph of your zodiac sign to find your date of birth, and down the side for your birth time (I have used Greenwich Mean Time). Where they cross is your Rising Sign. Don't forget to subtract an hour (or two) if appropriate for Summer Time.

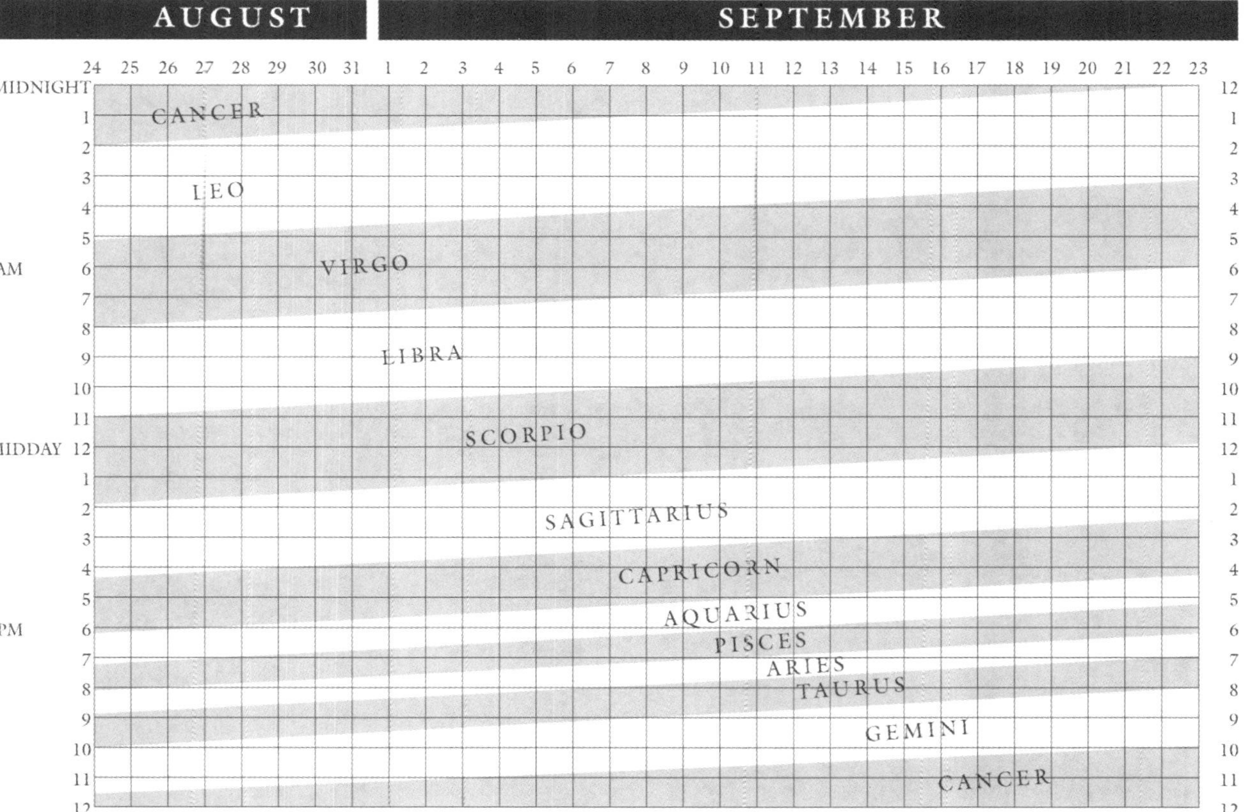
AUGUST
SEPTEMBER
MIDNIGHT
AM
MIDDAY
PM
CANCER
LEO
VIRGO
LIBRA
SCORPIO
SAGITTARIUS
CAPRICORN
AQUARIUS
PISCES
ARIES
TAURUS
GEMINI
CANCER

# THE ZODIAC, PLANETS AND CORRESPONDENCES

The Earth revolves around the Sun once every calendar year, so when viewed from Earth the Sun appears in a different part of the sky as the year progresses. In astrology, these parts of the sky are divided into the signs of the zodiac and this means that the signs are organised in a circle. The circle begins with Aries and ends with Pisces.

Taking the zodiac sign as a starting point, astrologers then work with all the positions of planets, stars and many other factors to calculate horoscopes and birth charts and tell us what the stars have in store for us.

The table below shows the planets and Elements for each of the signs of the zodiac. Each sign belongs to one of the four Elements: Fire, Air, Earth or Water. Fire signs are creative and enthusiastic; Air signs are mentally active and thoughtful; Earth signs are constructive and practical; Water signs are emotional and have strong feelings.

It also shows the metals and gemstones associated with, or corresponding with, each sign. The correspondence is made when a metal or stone possesses properties that are held in common with a particular sign of the zodiac.

Finally, the table shows the opposite of each star sign – this is the opposite sign in the astrological circle.

| Placed | Sign | Symbol | Element | Planet | Metal | Stone | Opposite |
|---|---|---|---|---|---|---|---|
| 1 | Aries | Ram | Fire | Mars | Iron | Bloodstone | Libra |
| 2 | Taurus | Bull | Earth | Venus | Copper | Sapphire | Scorpio |
| 3 | Gemini | Twins | Air | Mercury | Mercury | Tiger's Eye | Sagittarius |
| 4 | Cancer | Crab | Water | Moon | Silver | Pearl | Capricorn |
| 5 | Leo | Lion | Fire | Sun | Gold | Ruby | Aquarius |
| 6 | Virgo | Maiden | Earth | Mercury | Mercury | Sardonyx | Pisces |
| 7 | Libra | Scales | Air | Venus | Copper | Sapphire | Aries |
| 8 | Scorpio | Scorpion | Water | Pluto | Plutonium | Jasper | Taurus |
| 9 | Sagittarius | Archer | Fire | Jupiter | Tin | Topaz | Gemini |
| 10 | Capricorn | Goat | Earth | Saturn | Lead | Black Onyx | Cancer |
| 11 | Aquarius | Waterbearer | Air | Uranus | Uranium | Amethyst | Leo |
| 12 | Pisces | Fishes | Water | Neptune | Tin | Moonstone | Virgo |